1985

ENCYCLOPEDIA
OF U.S. COINS

A completely revised, updated edition

ENCYCLOPEDIA OF U.S. COINS

MORT REED

Foreword by Gilroy Roberts,
Former Chief Engraver with the U.S. Mint

HENRY REGNERY COMPANY · CHICAGO

To
my wife and daughter, Betty and Fronie,
the other two-thirds of this effort

CONTENTS

PART 1. FEDERAL SEALS AND COINAGE

Die Preparations. Die Sections. Polished Die. Design Laydown. Die and Reverse Art. The Basic Gravers. The Master Die. Hubbing. The Hub. The Working Die. Hand Stamping. Overdating. Rim Dies. Ornate Rims. The Janvier Lathe. The Modern Hub. The Kennedy Half-Dollar. Metals and Alloys. Table of Melting Points and Densities. Alloyed Metal. Ingot Compositions. Rolling. Blanking. Riddle and Polish. Upsetting. Annealing. Washing. Drying. Weighing. Inspection. Stamping and Reeding. Tabulation. Weighing and Shipping. Distribution. Wrapping. Boxing. The Coinage Act of 1965. The Coinage Act of 1970.

PART 2.   COINOLOGY

FOREWORD

A numismatist is defined as one who is skilled in numismatics, the science of coins and medals. Coins are an ever-present commodity in the daily lives of all of us, and such familiar, uncomplicated objects that we tend to take them for granted.

That there can be a science about these everyday, commonplace things seldom occurs to most of us. In the past there were always a few individuals who devoted much of their time and effort to the serious study and assembly of collections of coins. In more recent times, clubs and societies have formed, but these still represented a very small segment of society. Up until a few years ago, the bulk of their membership was limited to a few who were interested in miniature art, historians, certain scholars—and, of course, numismatists. Today, people in all walks of life are taking an active interest in this subject and, to a greater or lesser extent, becoming numismatists.

A considerable amount of literature and information has been contributed by numerous experts and scholars, but there still seems to be many misconceptions about coins and medals, particularly with respect to the methods of their manufacture and the causes of variations in them.

My own interest in this subject has, for the most part, been limited to artistry, design, and production. Since this is only part of a much more complex science, I can hardly be considered a numismatist. But during my many years of processing coins and medals for our government, as well as for private enterprise, I have met several of our country's noted experts in this field. Their dedication and enthusiasm have helped me to more fully appreciate the whole science of numismatics.

No doubt many of us do not stop to think about what is involved in research—in digging up long-forgotten information and finding authentic answers to puzzling questions; the countless hours going here and there, patiently searching through old records and dusty archives; the many blind alleys and disappointments.

The motivation is the possibility of turning up some significant bit of information. When the many long and seemingly fruitless searches do yield an elusive date or designer, it makes the effort ultimately rewarding.

Cowles Complete Encyclopedia of U.S. Coins is a welcome example of such perseverance and patience. It contains an unbelievable amount of absolutely authentic and greatly valued numismatic information. It has well fulfilled its author's purpose in that it is a serious reference book for the numismatist, a guide for the beginning collector, and a spellbinding tale of the nation's entire money system.

Gilroy Roberts

Former Chief Engraver with the U. S. Mint; Chairman of the Board of Directors of the Franklin Mint, Yeadon, Pennsylvania; and designer and engraver of the Kennedy Half-Dollar.

INTRODUCTION

The author of this book is a man of many talents. He can illustrate; he can write, and he is an expert on coins. Put these considerable and compatible talents together, add a dash of *savoir faire*, mix well with printer's ink, and one of the leading contributors to the enjoyment and education of coin collectors emerges—Mort Reed.

Mr. Reed resides in Wooster, Ohio. In his studio he prepares his nationally syndicated newspaper column, "Money Clips," and creates for the coin collectors' weekly newspaper, *Coin World,* one of its most popular features, "Coinology." Hundreds of his fans clip and save "Coinology," which is a handy illustrated panel.

Mr. Reed draws on nearly four decades of personal experiences as a coin collector and numismatist, and he has never lost the aesthetics. He is devoted to his responsibility to the reading public. Many times we have heard him pose a question concerning the effect a point of order or procedure might have on the reader and then turn to his drawing board to stress his interpretation of the good and the sensible in coin-collecting practices.

We know of no one with more concern for technical accuracy. The instruments he uses to accomplish his evangelism are his "Coinology" panel in *Coin World* and his newspaper column "Money Clips," each of which reach literally thousands of readers each week.

This book is, in reality, a bonus, since it was compiled in addition to Mr. Reed's daily task as an illustrator and writer. If it serves its purpose to any degree, then those waking hours of extra endeavor were well spent. His first book, *Odd and Curious,* was a collection of original *Coin World* panels that dealt exclusively with the unusual media of exchange used throughout the world, and is one of the classic references in the specialized field of numismatics and in the science of coin collecting.

In *Cowles Complete Encyclopedia of U.S. Coins,* Mr. Reed elects to stay within the area of United States numismatics, and with a mannerism that will broaden the various concepts, to reach both the informed and the uninformed in and out of the numismatic world. He contends that a thorough knowledge of American coinage is far too valuable an asset to receive anything less than our fullest attention, an attitude with which we heartily agree. He has researched, checked, doublechecked, and contacted authorities from key Treasury Department people to denomination specialists scattered all over the country. He hoped to bring the facts to his readers—which he did—and he tried to illuminate those facts in the most unique and understandable manner. In this, too, he has succeeded.

We at *Coin World* listened to his dreams, his aims, and his concerns —all of which centered upon those things that were for the betterment of the collector and the industry—and we encouraged him. That is our small measure of credit for this fine book.

Margo Russell, Editor
Coin World

PURPOSE AND ACKNOWLEDGMENTS

Cowles Complete Encyclopedia of U.S. Coins is primarily intended as a central source of authoritative reference material for whatever use such information is required. It is not channelled to any single group with more than a normal interest in coins, but it does lean heavily on knowledge gained from professional numismatists.

Until recently, the desire for more than a basic knowledge of our coinage was limited to those few with the wherewithal to collect coins as a hobby; the research necessary to support that hobby was considered a major pursuit in the enjoyment. Today all that has changed. The fast-moving events in domestic and foreign monetary systems have received more than their fair share of publicity with the result that the general public has become extremely coin-conscious.

While a majority of the noncollecting public is keenly aware of the fact that a coin can have two values—its intended value and its collector's value—they are not sufficiently versed in matters of type and design identification and few find little concilation upon submitting their inquiries to the local "expert." For that reason they expect, and even demand, some relief for their frustration. Rightfully so, for here and there a treasure can bring some measure of fame and fortune. Hopefully, this encyclopedia will help the uninformed to determine the extent of his holdings.

In addition to encouraging a deeper enthusiasm for our coinage, this work should be of particular interest to members of the bar and the banking professions who are concerned with the appraisal and evaluation of coins and collections involved in estates or as collateral assets. Its format was purposely arranged to assist an appraiser in establishing the proper identity and condition of a coin.

To reduce the hazards of miscalculation, each coin illustration is maintained at a uniform size of two inches regardless of denomination to facilitate easier recognition of the qualifying features that could mean the difference between high and nominal value. Since there is a possibility that a high-value coin may be either an altered or counterfeit piece, one section has been devoted to a list of the unauthorized coins known to exist by denomination, date, design, metal, and method of fabrication, as well as processes for immediate verification.

This brings up another purpose of the book. While the responsibility for confiscation of an unauthorized coin and prosecution of the offender rests entirely with the United States Secret Service, preliminary investigation is within the jurisdiction of the local civil authority until it has been determined that an unlawful situation does exist. Here the encyclopedia serves to shorten the orientation period for the investigating officer by making all that is known of a coin available in one bound volume. In addition to visually aiding the officer, the properties considered by the United States Mint as naturally essential in an authorized coin are dealt with individually, as well as those properties peculiar to an unauthorized coin.

For convenience only, one section relates verbatim the counterfeit and forgery laws and penalties and the alteration and defacing laws and their penalties, along with certain acts considered equally unlawful although indirectly associated with violations of the coinage laws.

In short, every effort has been made to provide an answer for any question that may arise regarding the coinage of the United States, with the exception of possible market values. Speculation, prices, and investments are the responsibility of the numismatic industry.

The encyclopedic format is in the interest of brevity, and to maintain an understandable continuity from the origin of our coinage to the many end uses other than as circulating mediums. Personal theories have been purposely kept to a minimum except where it was necessary to clarify a point. Particular care has been taken to avoid controversy, but where fact may conflict with theory, the fact as given must stand because of its authenticated background.

The mintage figures used in the specifics for each coin have been printed by permission of the Whitman Division of the Western Publishing Company, Inc., Racine, Wisconsin, publishers of *A Guide Book of United States Coins,* by Richard Yeoman. They are the result of intensive study conducted in the interest of better numismatics. The figures are believed to be more accurate than official mint records, which are often incomplete.

Many U. S. government agencies have graciously contributed to the preparation of this work. I am particularly grateful to the Bureau of the Mint, the United States Secret Service, the Bureau of Engraving and Printing, and the Office of the President of the United States. Without their generous assistance, much of the technical material would be less than authoritative. The most important contribution to the overall effort must be acknowledged as coming from the numismatic society itself. Most appreciated was their encouragement to produce this encyclopedia. Special gratitude dictates individual acknowledgements to Margo Russell, Editor, and Oliver Amos, Publisher, of *Coin World,* the coin collectors' newspaper. Without them and their fine staff of editors, perplexities would have mounted upon perplexities.

I am exceedingly appreciative of the most generous cooperation on the parts of Kenneth E. Bressett of the Western Publishing Company; Don Taxay, author of *U.S. Mint and Coinage;* and Clifford Mishler, Numismatic Editor of Krause Publications. More thanks to Q. David Bowers and James Ruddy of Bowers and Ruddy Galleries; Virgil Hancock and the trustees of American Numismatic Authentication Trust; the American Numismatic Association; and the American Numismatic Society.

In a very special way, I shall always be indebted to Gilroy Roberts for his encouragement and inspiring foreword; James Hamer, metallurgical engineer with Astro Metallurgical; Robert A. Jones, Head of the Technical Services Division and Dr. William F. Kieffer, Professor of Chemistry, both of the College of Wooster; Robert R. Metz and the Newspaper Enterprise Association; Lee Martin and James Miller of *Coinage* magazine; and last but certainly not least an extra special thanks to the many readers who have offered friendly but constructive criticism pending a second edition.

Mort Reed

P.S. Second Edition—

Nothing justifies a second edition more than the knowledge that the first edition is no longer the last word.

GLOSSARY

Accidental Rarity. An improperly struck coin.

Alloyed. Composed of one or more pure metals.

Alloyed Melt. The process of homogenizing metals by melting.

Altered. A genuine coin altered or defaced to represent another of special value.

Annealing. Softening hardened metal by a given heat and cooling process.

Annulet. A circle of five-point stars encompassing the President's Seal.

Antidated Pieces. Coins struck and dated after the date of regular issue.

Argent. Heraldic term for white or silver, which signify purity or innocence.

Armorial. The design and attitude of a family crest or seal.

Arms. Heraldic term for a family seal or crest. (State or federal seal.)

Authenticate. Verify or establish as genuine or as represented.

Authorized Coin. A coin that has been issued by authority of the director of the mint and that meets all the requirements of the prevailing coinage act.

Azure. Heraldic term for blue.

Base Metal. A crude or low form of metal, usually leaded.

Beaded. A continuous border pattern of beads.

Bit. The eighth part of a Spanish dollar.

Black Lead. Graphite or plumbago. (A conductive coating.)

Blanking Press. Mint machine used to stamp or cut coin blanks.

Bullion. Any unrefined precious metal, or refined and uncoined. In bars.

Burnishing. A process of making smooth by rubbing with a tool.

Cabinet Pieces. Coins in a collector's coin cabinet. Mint showpieces.

Cast Metal. Metal coin or bar formed from molten metal.

Cavity. The recessed impression of a coin in a die.

Central Device. The main configuration on either side of a coin.

Chain Mail. An article of clothing of united chain links. (Mesh.)

Chased. Describing an object formed by the art of "chasing" with a tool.

Chevrons. In heraldry, the honorable ordinary of two house rafters.

Chief. The upper part of a shield. (The blue area of the U.S. shield.)

Circulating Medium. A nation's coinage issued for general circulation.

Circumscribed. Drawn around in a circular fashion.

Circumvented. Closed in or encircled.

Clad Coinage. The term for our present sandwich coins with a copper center.

Coat of Arms. Heraldic term for a family seal or crest.

Coinage. The whole of a nation's coins.

Coin of the Realm. The circulating medium of a nation.

Coinologist. One skilled in the science of coins and medals.

COINOLOGY. The science of coins. (Registered trademark of author.)

Configuration. The outline or external shape of a device or symbol.

Conically. Brought to a point. An inverted cone.

Constellation. A collection or mass of stars.

Coronet. A tiara or female headpiece, plain or beaded.

Counterfeit. A fabricated illegal coin.

Counterstamp. Usually the official stamp of one nation on the coinage of another to make it the coin of the realm.

Crest. Heraldic term for a symbol within a seal or coat of arms.

Crosslet. In numismatics, the angular and horizontal lines as in Figure 4.

Cupronickel. An alloy of 75% copper and 25% nickel.

Curvature of the Field. The recess or concave indentation of a coin's surface.

Cutting the Date. The hand process of affixing the date to a die.

Dead-smooth File. A rasp for smoothing roughened steel.

Density. The thickness or compactness of the molecular structure of metal.

Denticles. A type of border pattern.

Design Properties. The symbols and features in a specified design.

Device. A symbol or group of symbols emblematic of a concept or principle. A design heraldic in nature.

Dexter. Heraldic term for the right-hand side of a shield.

Die Blank. The die section of steel prepared for impression of a design.

Die Section. The short length of steel used to make a coin die.

Disclosed. Heraldic term describing an eagle with spread but inverted wings pointing downward.

Displayed Proper. Heraldic term for an eagle with upraised wings.

Double-struck. A coin with part of its design doubled.

Eagle Volant. Heraldic term for an eagle in free flight.

Ebullition. Bubbling action of water due to sudden application of heat.

Effigy. The likeness or image of a person as portrayed on a coin.

Electrotype. A metallic impression transferred from an original by means of electric deposition.

Embattlement Border. A particular border arrangement.

Embay. To enclose or confine to a specific area.

England's Britannia. The seated female figure on Britain's coinage.

Engrailed. A particular border pattern.

Erasing the Date. Grinding the date's digits from the hubbing die.

Escutcheon. Heraldic term for a shield.

Exergue. A space for the date in the base of a coin. (Usually on the reverse.)

Fake. Any coin that is not genuine or has been altered.

Field. The surface area of a coin containing the inscription and device.

Fillet. A small ribbon or string used to contain the hair.

Fineness. A reference to the purity of a precious metal.

Fissures. A small crack or imperfection in a coining die or die blank.

Fleur-de-lis. Heraldry for the lily, a symbol of royalty.

Fusing. Joining two metals in a permanent bond.

Galvano. A metallic reproduction of the model for a coin made from the model. Usually of the same size.

Georgius Rex. Latin for King George, head of the United Kingdom.

Glory. Heraldic term for a halo of cloud puffs surrounding a symbol.

Gules. Heraldic term for red. Depicted by vertical lines.

Hand Lapping. The process of finishing a steel surface with an oil stone by hand. Polishing.

Hardening. The process of hardening steel by a heat treatment.

Hard Money. Used in this book to mean coins.

Height of the Device. The thickness of the image on a coin as gauged from the surface or field.

Heraldic. From heraldry. Describing the science of studying and recording the armorial designs of families and governments.

Heraldic Eagle. An eagle with legs and wings apart in a displayed manner. Bearing other symbols.

Herculean Pillars. The design on the reverse of a Piece of Eight.

High Value. The value of a coin excessive of its normal value.

"Holey" Dollar. The various Spanish dollars with their centers removed to establish them as coin of the realm for another nation.

Hub. The cameo or positive impression of an intaglio or negative die used to mass-produce working dies. The design in relief.

Impression. The reverse likeness of a die or hub impressed into any material, usually into another die for stamping.

In Base. The bottom of the coin. (Below the device.)

Incuse. Process of impressing the design below a coin's surface.

Ingot. A mass of pure or alloyed metal in a standard form of bar or slab. Molded from molten metal to a particular form.

Inscribed. Engraved or stamped lettering. Usually the motto or LIBERTY.

Intaglio Impression. See **Incuse.**

Intermediate Model. A stage or reduction from the original model's size to a more workable size larger than the finished coin.

Interposing. Standing between or separating two objects or wreaths.

Intrinsic value. The internal or actual metal worth of a coin.

Issuing Authority. The issuing government or a recognized agency of the government. (The Federal Reserve System.)

Janvier Lathe. An instrument for the reduction of a design from the original size of the model to the coin size of the die.

Knurling. A common reference to the vertical milling in a rim die for coins with a reeded edge.

Laid On. As used in this book, the application of a numeral or letter to one coin after removal from another.

Legal Tender. An official term implying the status of coin and currency, making it acceptable in payments of all debts.

Legend. The area around the inner part of a coin's border occupied by an inscription as provided by a coinage act.

Lettered. Describing the edge of a coin bearing its value.

Liberty Abstract. Any effigy of an unrecognizable person to imply the figure of Liberty. (Emblematic of Liberty.)

Liberty, Specific. An effigy of a recognizable person whose contributions to democracy made him a symbol of freedom and liberty.

Lifted. As used in this book, the actual removal of a numeral or letter from one coin for the purpose of applying it to another.

Lost Wax. A casting process of forcing the metal into the design.

Malleability. Capacity to be shaped, as in softer or more pliable metal.

Maltese Cross. A cross with its four outer surfaces dovetailed to form two spiked corners to each surface, or eight to the cross.

Master Die. One never used for striking coins. Usually the die used to raise a hub that will in turn make working dies.

Mercury Head. A visual terminology for the Winged Liberty Cap Dime of 1916. A numismatic reference.

Milling Machine. A mint machine for applying the reedings to a coin.

Minor Coinage. The One-Cent and Five-Cent Pieces.

Mintage. The whole of a year's coin production. (". . . the year's mintage.")

Mint Sets. Uncirculated specimen of each coin issued for general circulation.

Monarchial Principal of Eulogizing. The manner in which the kings of a monarchy were honored on their countries' coinage.

Monogram. A signature usually consisting of one or two initials superimposed one on the other, or in some similar manner, to represent a personal mark.

Motifs. Modes or formats. Organized designs with purposeful patterns.

Mullet. A five- or six-pointed star, usually with a pierced center.

Multi-bow. A ribbon knot tied with more than one bow.

Multiple-die Holder. The head or hammer of a press designed to hold several coin dies at one time.

Multiplying Press. Any press used for hubbing working dies.

Multi-punch Press. A press capable of cutting or punching more than one coin blank at a time.

Negative Impression. The cavity or reverse of the original design.

New-die Proofs. First coins struck of working dies. Not proofs.

Nonfunctional Design. The star or group of symbols without legal or heraldic meaning. Usually an engraver's choice.

Numismatics. The study of the arts and sciences of coins and coinage.

Numismatist. Same as coinologist.

Obverse. The face or "front" of a coin.

Or. Heraldic term for gold or yellow.

Ornate. Fancy. A design with excessive scroll work.

Ornithologist. An expert in the study of birds.

Overvalued. By overvaluing their coinage, many countries prevented the export of their precious metals.

Paleways (Paleys). Heraldic term for stripes.

Pantographic Instruments. A machine employing the pantographic principal in transferring the design of a model to the coining die. (A portrait lathe such as the *Janvier*.)

Pattée Cross. A cross with four flat surfaces often confused with Maltese cross.

Pedestal of the Neck. The lower sculptured edge on the neck of a bust.

Periphery Line. The circumference line of a coin or die.

Pesos, Piastres, and Pieces of Eight. Terms for Spanish dollars.

Phrygian Slave's Cap. A loose-fitting head cover used to signal Roman citizens that the wearer was a freed slave.

Pileus. Same as Phrygian Slave's Cap.

Planchets. Coin flans or blanks.

Plastilene. A form of modeling plaster or clay used by engravers and sculptors to make the model for a coin or medal.

Portrait Lathe. Similar to the Janvier lathe and the pantograph.

Positive Expression. Another way of describing a cameo or hub design.

Pound Sterling. The unit of account for Great Britain.

Proof. The special condition of a coin expressly prepared with a mirror finish for the purpose of displays, gifts to foreign dignitaries, and coin collectors. Struck hydraulically.

Prototype. The original model for the finished design or coin.

Radially. In a curved or arched manner.

Radial Markings. A border pattern using a series of parallel markings on the rim edge of the coin.

Radiants. Like the rays from the sun. Spikelike.

Radiating Glory. A glory with indications of rays piercing the edges.

Radical. With no definite pattern. Without uniformity.

Rarity. The quantitative condition of a coin. A limited number.

Real. A Spanish denominational term.

Reeded. The pattern of a coin's edge. Transverse reedings.

Relief. The extent of depth to a design. High is deep; low is shallow.

Reverse. The back or "rear" of a coin.

Riddle. The shaking process used to remove foreign particles from freshly cut coin blanks.

Rim. The obverse and reverse surface of the edge of a coin. See **Upsetting.**

Roman Liberatus. The seated female figure on Roman coinage and art.

Scarcity. The quantitative condition of a coin somewhat more available than those considered rare.

Scroll. The banner or ribbon on United States coins. Usually bears one of the mottoes.

Serif. The horizontal finish line on a printed letter of the alphabet. Generally found on the top and bottom of a vertical letter. A continuous serif continues from one letter to the next without the conventional break in between.

Serrations. Misnomer applied to certain border patterns or the edge of a silver coin.

Sinister. Heraldic term for the left-hand side of a shield.

Sinking. The process of impressing the image from a hub to a die.

Specific Gravity. A metallurgical process to determine the density of metal.

Specifics. The precise particulars. Exact properties.

Specimen. An example or sample. The proof impression of two dies.

Spectrograph. A scientific means of determining the composition of a metal incorporating the use of X ray.

Star. A five- or six-point symbol. A mullet.

Supporting Appointments. Those symbols that surround a main device and contribute to the general motif.

Sweated On. As used in this book, a means of soldering a device, numeral, or letter from one coin to another for the purpose of defrauding.

Talons. The claws of an eagle.

To Raise. To bring up or to cause a design to be cameoed on the surface of a die. A process requiring more than one strike.

Transverse (ly). At right angles to or on an approximate 90-degree angle. Across to the right or left.

Truncation. The lower edge or finished part of a sculptured bust. The scroll cutoff above the shoulder line.

Union Shield. The shield of the United States regardless of its overall configuration.

Upsetting. The process of turning up the edge or rim of a coin.

Wood Belfry. The beam that holds a bell.

Working Die. The die used to actually strike a coin.

PART I

FEDERAL SEALS AND COINAGE

CHAPTER I

FEDERAL SEALS

The Great Seal of the United States And Its Evolution
(Reproductions from the Original drawings)

The First Design, Submitted in 1776

On July 4, 1776, immediately following the signing of the Declaration of Independence, three members of the original five-man committee responsible for drafting that instrument were chosen to prepare an appropriate sign of sovereignty for the newly formed government of the United States of America. This august body consisted of Benjamin Franklin, Thomas Jefferson, and John Adams.

They submitted an obverse design containing a center shield laden with heraldic symbols and flanked on the right by a figure of Liberty holding a staff topped by the Phrygian slave's cap, and on the left by a figure of Justice, without her blindfold, holding a pair of balance scales. Above was the eye of Providence, and below, the motto, E PLURIBUS UNUM.

Around the device an interseries of circles was surmounted by thirteen shields, each bearing the initial letter of one of the original thirteen colonies. An inscription in the border belt read SEAL OF THE UNITED STATES OF AMERICA and bore the date in Roman numerals MDCCLXXVI (1776).

The reverse is described as Pharaoh, crowned, and sitting in a chariot, his sword passing through the divided waters of the Red Sea in pursuit of the Israelites. Rays from a pillar of fire guide Moses on the shore as he extends his arm to close the sea over Pharaoh. A circumscribed motto reads— REBELLION TO TYRANTS IS OBEDIENCE TO GOD.

Three components survived the seal's rejection: the motto, the eye of Providence, and the Phrygian slave's cap.

The Second Design, Submitted in 1780

Congress and the new administration functioned for four years without the benefit of a seal of authority. On March 25, 1780, a second committee was appointed to resolve the problem; it comprised John Scott of Virginia, James Lovell of Massachusetts, and William Houston of New Jersey.

They suggested for the obverse a flaming shield in the center, occupied by seven white and six red diagonal stripes with two opposing fields of blue, and flanked on the right by a Roman soldier and on the left by Liberty holding an olive branch in her left hand. Imprinted above was a glory (a radiant halo) of thirteen five-point stars, and below, a scroll bearing the unlikely motto of BELLO VEL PACI for "Let there be war or peace." An inscription between the inner and outer borders read THE GREAT SEAL OF THE UNITED STATES OF AMERICA.

On the reverse a seated figure of Liberty held a staff topped with the familiar Phrygian slave's cap, with the legend SEMPER ("eternal") running above. The date, in Roman numerals, was in the exergue, the space below the device.

This suggestion was also rejected, but we should note the eight features, used in two interpretations of a coat of arms, that appear on either the paper currency or coinage of the United States today. Seven are components —the seated figure of Liberty, the eye of Providence, the five-point star, the motto E PLURIBUS UNUM, the Phrygian slave's cap, the glory of thirteen stars, and the use of Roman numerals for the date. The eighth feature is the thirteen-stripe arrangement in the shield.

The Third Design, Submitted in 1782

Six years after the signing of the Declaration of Independence the matter of a national seal was no closer to reality than it had been on the afternoon of July 4, 1776. Six men had worked on two devices, both of which had been rejected, and the situation was assuming the proportions of an emergency.

On May 14, 1782, Congress selected three gentlemen with a combined knowledge of heraldry and numismatics, hoping this step would lead to some measure of success. Arthur Middleton and Edward Rutledge, both of South Carolina, were chosen, conceivably for their advanced understanding of heraldry; and Elias Boudinot of New Jersey, for his interest in medals and coins. Boudinot's expertise in this field eventually secured him an appointment as third director of the mint, a post he held from October 28, 1795, to June, 1805.

Boudinot influenced the committee's decision to retain the services of William Barton, a Philadelphia attorney with background in the art of numismatics, who served also as consultant to the board charged with establishing the mint and a national coinage system. It was largely through his efforts that the third design ultimately evolved into a seal.

The eagle emerged as the final device. The reverse, with its unfinished thirteen-step (for the thirteen colonies) pyramid and eye of Providence, was almost entirely acceptable with a few adjustments in the art and complete replacement of the mottoes.

The Fourth Design, Also Submitted in 1782

One man with a more-than-casual knowledge of the proceedings to this point was Charles Thompson, Secretary to the Congress and a fairly well-versed student of heraldry. He took it upon himself to advance a few suggestions on paper that eventually caught the attention of Mr. Barton. Thompson used the eagle shown at the top of the third design's device and arranged it to occupy the entire area of the field. The eagle's talons held a bundle of thirteen arrows and an olive branch, and a shield of red and white chevrons crossed its breast.

Mr. Barton revised the comprehensive sketch made by Secretary Thompson by changing the chevrons to thirteen red and white vertical stripes; adding the motto E Pluribus Unum; inserting the glory of thirteen stars; and fixing the number of arrows to thirteen.

On June 20, 1782, the new seal was adopted by Congress. No one person is responsible for its completion because it contains at least two features from each previous suggestion, which rightfully makes it the work of Benjamin Franklin, Thomas Jefferson, John Adams, James Lovell, John Scott, William Houston, Arthur Middleton, Edward Rutledge, Elias Boudinot, William Barton, and Charles Thompson.

It should be understood that, although these gentlemen were the combined force behind the various designs, the features finally used were mere suggestions that had appeared first on coin and paper currency issued by several of the states.

The Legal and Illegal Seal

Following approval and final adoption by Congress, an engraving of the obverse only was ordered into service, and during the period preceding the formation of a state department and the appointment of its executive officer, the Secretary to Congress was charged with the safekeeping of the engraving. The reason for not cutting the reverse is not on record. Orders for reverse engravings were issued in 1782, 1789, 1841, 1883, 1884, and again in 1885, but it wasn't until the Treasury Department issued the 1935 one-dollar reverse that the reverse of the Great Seal made its public appearance.

Although the features had been approved and adopted, no specifics were ever laid down to control an engraver's interpretation of those features with respect to their proper arrangement on the seal. One seal cut in 1782 was, naturally, the express design approved by Congress, but certain latitudes were assumed by the engraver in 1841 that caused it to be officially declared "illegal." It lacked the thirteen arrows prescribed in the adoption, and the stripes were not proportionate in width—red to white.

In 1884 an obverse was cut in keeping with the rules governing the application of symbols, and by an Act of Congress in 1903, it was determined that henceforth all new engravings would be recut from the original.

Approved November 11, 1966
The Great Seal of the United States
Use of likeness prohibited.

Public Law 89-807
89th Congress, S. 1770
November 11, 1966

An Act

To amend title 18 of the United States Code so as to prohibit the use of likenesses of the Great Seal of the United States falsely to indicate Federal agency, sponsorship, or approval.

Be it enacted by the Senate and House of Representatives of the United States of America in Congress assembled, That (a) chapter 33 of title 18, United States Code, is amended by adding at the end thereof the following new section:

§ 713. Use of the Great Seal of the United States.

"Whoever knowingly displays any printed or other likeness of the Great Seal of the United States, on any facsimile thereof, in, or in connection with, any advertisement, circular, book, pamphlet, or other publication, play, motion picture, telecast, or other production for the purpose of conveying and in a manner reasonably calculated to convey the false impression that all or any part of such advertisement, circular, book, pamphlet, or other publication, play, motion picture, telecast, or other production, is sponsored or approved by the Government of the United States, or any department, agency, or instrumentality thereof, shall be fined not more than $250 or imprisoned not more than six months, or both."

(b) The analysis of Chapter 33 of Title 18, United States Code, immediately preceding Section 701 of such title is amended by adding at the end thereof:

"713 Use of likenesses of the Great Seal of the United States."

The Great Seal of the United States
Its Legal Description

Arms. Paleways of thirteen pieces, *argent* and *gules;* a chief, *azure;* the escutcheon on the breast of the American Eagle displayed proper, holding in his dexter talon an olive branch, in his sinister a bundle of thirteen arrows, all proper, and in his beak a scroll, inscribed with the motto E PLURIBUS UNUM.

Crest. Over the head of the eagle, which appears above the escutcheon, a glory, *or,* breaking through the cloud, proper, surrounding thirteen stars, forming a constellation, *argent,* on an *azure* field.

Reverse. A pyramid unfinished. In the zenith, an eye in a triangle, surrounded by a glory proper. Over the eye these words, ANNUIT COEPTIS. On the base of the pyramid the numerical letters MDCCLXXVI. And underneath the following motto, NOVUS ORDO SECLOREM.

The engravings of the Great Seal of the United States were prepared by the Bureau of Engraving and Printing, Washington, D.C.

The Seal of the President of the United States
Its Legal Description

The coat of arms of the President of the United States shall be of the following design:

Shield: Paleways, or vertical equal bars, of thirteen pieces, argent and gules (red); the upper part of the shield, or chief, in azure, set upon the breast of an American eagle holding in his dexter talon an olive branch, in his sinister a bundle of thirteen arrows all proper, and in his beak a white scroll inscribed E PLURIBUS UNUM, in sable.

Crest: Behind and above the eagle a radiating glory with an arc of thirteen cloud puffs proper, and a constellation of thirteen mullets, or stars, argent. The whole is surrounded by white stars arranged in the form of an annulet, or ring, with one point of each star outward on the imaginary radiating center lines. The number of stars must conform to the number of stars in the union of the flag of the United States as established by Chapter 1 of Title 4 of the United States Code.

The Seal of the President of the United States shall consist of the coat of arms encircled by the words SEAL OF THE PRESIDENT OF THE UNITED STATES.

The Seal of the President of the United States is his personal property during his tenure in office and its use is restricted under Title 18 of the United States Code. It is used here with the express permission of President Richard M. Nixon.

Seal of The Department of the Treasury
Its Legal Description

In 1778 the Continental Congress appointed John Witherspoon, Richard Henry Lee, and Gouverneur Morris to design seals for the departments of the Navy and Treasury. Although the committee reported on the Navy seal in 1780, it did not submit a detailed account for the Treasury seal. Francis Hopkins is considered the designer but no official explanation for the motto, which embraces all of North America, is available—the motto, THESAUR AMER SEPTENT SIGII, is translated as "Seal of the Treasury of North America."

Treasury Department Seal

Arms: A chevron azure, between a pair of balanced scales in chief, and in base, a key ward downward to dexter, both azure, with thirteen mullets argent on the chevron.

The arms are displayed upon a circular background of American blue; within a legend ring surrounding the arms, and circumscribed by two concentric white rings, there appears the inscription THE DEPARTMENT OF THE TREASURY, in white capital letters, and the date, 1789.

CHAPTER II

THE ORIGIN OF
UNITED STATES COINAGE

The Spanish Milled Dollar

The Spanish milled dollar is probably one of the most, if not the most, celebrated coins in the annals of international hard money. Its extremely high silver content made it a preferred specie in bids for control over Oriental trade, and is largely responsible for a general adjustment of all world monetary systems.

Many countries found the Piece of Eight an ideal substitute or subsidiary coin, and in this role it smoothed the troubled waters of internal financial problems. During the late eighteenth and early nineteenth century, England found herself facing a silver shortage that would destroy her banking system unless hoarded silver was placed back in circulation. To offset certain disaster, thousands of Spanish dollars, seized from ships of the Spanish merchant fleet, were counterstamped with the likeness of King George III and circulated as coin of the realm.

The new dollar was received by the public resentfully but almost immediately a potentially dangerous situation was diverted to one of relative calm among the bankers. Eventually the Spanish coins were redeemed by the Bank of England and converted into bullion to be reissued as sovereign coinage.

Fractional Use of the Spanish Milled Dollar

A fractional application of the Spanish milled dollar by the colonists was the origin of many terms identified with our current denominations. The English referred to a real as a "bit," a usage that was subsequently carried over into American commercial outlets and on into the marketplaces until it became a standard term of reference.

Since "piece of eight" describes a coin of eight units or pieces, it is only natural that half a dollar should be referred to as four reals or four bits and, by the same token, a quartered section of two reals was called two bits. Half of a quartered section was a real or one bit and, divided equally, a bit produced two picayunes valued at six and one-half cents each.

The Long and Short Bits

When a quartered section was divided unequally on a forty-to-sixty proportion of the quarter section, the smaller piece was a short bit valued at ten cents and the larger piece was a long bit valued at fifteen cents.

13

New Orleans

Certain areas in the United States found other variations of the Spanish dollar more suitable to their particular needs.

New Orleans counterstamped the quartered sections and issued them as hard-times tokens.

Prince Edward Island

Treasury authorities used the entire coin by counterstamping GR in large letters for "Georgius Rex" over the figure 5 denoting the redeemable value in shillings.*

The "holey" dollar with slightly more than half of its center removed was another form used by the Prince Edward Island authorities.

* Authenticity questionable.

New South Wales
Australia

In 1813 this government removed a portion of the center of a piece of eight and impressed the area around the hole with the inscription NEW SOUTH WALES 1813.

Grenada, West Indies

The value of the Spanish milled dollar made it subject to export. To discourage this practice, Grenada divided it into eleven overvalued sections, and stamped each with a large incuse letter ɢ.

Curaçao, West Indies

Curaçao authorities also overvalued the Spanish dollar and cut it into five equal sections, each bearing the counterstamp of a rose.

Madagascar

Madagascar chopped the silver coins of all nations into small fragments and transacted business by weighing proper amounts of the mixed pieces.

In time the Spanish milled dollar was used to represent a fractional system of units with the smallest fraction equal to 1/72 or ten grains of rice.

The Island of St. Lucia

Using the French system of account, St. Lucia authorities cut the milled dollar into three parallel divisions and stamped each with the counterstamp of St. Lucia.

The value of the center (and larger) piece was three times that of the two side pieces.

British Guiana

A two-in-one adaptation of the Spanish dollar is also a form of the ring dollars used in parts of the West Indies and New South Wales.

Both pieces were used as money. Each was stamped with its particular value and the letters E. & D. for the colonies of Essequibo and Demerara.

The Shield of Spain

The shield of Charles and Joanna was quartered, showing the castle of Castile and the Lions of Leon with a small pomegranate of Grenada in the middle base.

When Philip, first of the Bourbon kings, assumed the throne, he had the shield redesigned to display the three fleurs-de-lis of the Bourbons in the center.

Popular acceptance of the Spanish milled dollar, both at home and abroad, convinced Congress that the new dollar or unit of the United States should be identical in every respect to the Spanish dollar, except, of course, for the design. A Congressional recommendation provided ". . . for the coinage of dollars or units, each to be of the value of a Spanish milled dollar, as the same is now current. . . ."

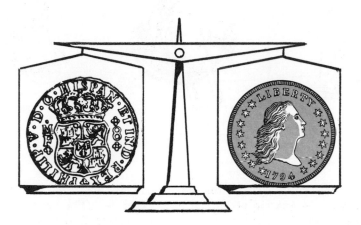

To accommodate both gold and silver interests, it was decided to create a double or bimetal standard with one part of gold equal to fifteen parts of silver—a fifteen-to-one ratio suitable for establishing the value of either the gold or silver unit.

To determine the silver content of a new dollar, it was necessary to first ascertain its value in gold. This was known in the marketplaces to be 24¾ grain of .916⅔ fine gold. Applying the unit ratio of fifteen-to-one, it followed that the value of a Spanish dollar was fifteen times 24¾ or .371¼ grains of .892⅖ fine silver. Properly alloyed, the gross weight of the new United States dollar was fixed at 416 grains—exactly that of the Spanish milled dollar.

"If we determine that a dollar is one unit, we must say with precision what a dollar is."

Thomas Jefferson

The Dollar Sign

Unlike the British symbol for the pound sterling, the dollar sign is not an official designation of United States currency. The sign does appear on certain types of federal revenue and fee stamps, and it is part of the design on no more than two pieces of paper currency of large denomination, but has never been used on a coin or paper currency of denominations issued for general circulation.

Contrary to popular belief, the dollar sign—whether the large letter s is superimposed on, or by a single or double vertical bar—is not a derivative of the Herculean pillars on the Spanish dollar, nor is it a monogram composed of the letters u and s.

The monogram is used extensively by agencies of the federal government, particularly the Bureau of Engraving and Printing, in the production of documents, fee stamps, paper currency and other forms of federal obligations, but never as a symbol of currency.

Dr. Florian Cajori, in his "History of Mathematical Notations,"* gives a detailed report of his years of researching this symbol and the results, which show that the dollar sign is actually a modification of the old Mexican sign P^8 for pesos, piastres, and pieces of eight.

$$P^8 \quad P \quad \$ \quad \$ \quad \$ \quad \$ \quad \$$$

* *The Numismatist,* August, 1929.

CHAPTER III

THE FIRST UNITED STATES COINAGE SYSTEM

THE FIRST COINAGE ACT

By the Act of April 2, 1792, Congress created the first national coinage system for the United States, established the value of a dollar and a unit, and provided for the production of a circulating medium.

Sections 1 thru 8 dealt with the enactments authorizing the erection and operation of a mint and supporting facilities.

Section 9

"And be it further enacted. That there shall be from time to time struck and coined at the said mint, coins of gold, silver and copper, of the following denominations, values and descriptions, viz:

"EAGLES—Each to be of the value of ten dollars or units, and to contain two hundred forty-seven grains and four eighths of a grain of pure, or two hundred and seventy grains of standard gold.

(Half and Quarter Eagle in exact proportions.)

"DOLLARS OR UNITS—Each to be of the value of a Spanish milled dollar as the same is now current, and to contain three hundred and seventy-one grains and four-sixteenths parts of a grain of pure, or four hundred and sixteen grains of standard silver.

(Half-Dollars, Quarter Dollars, Dimes and Half Dimes in exact proportions.)

"CENTS—Each to be of the value of the one hundredth part of a dollar, and to contain eleven pennyweights of copper.

(Half Cents in exact proportion.)"

Table of Values

Metal	Denomination	Value	Weight in Grains		Fineness
			Fine	Standard	
Gold	Eagle	$10	247½	270	.916⅔
	Half Eagle	$5	123¾	135	.916⅔
	Quarter Eagle	$2½	61⅞	67½	.916⅔
Silver	Dollar or Unit	$1	371¼	416	.892⅖
	Half-Dollar	50¢	185⅝	208	.892⅖
	Quarter Dollar	25¢	92 13/16	104	.892⅖
	Disme (Pronounced "dime")	10¢	37⅛	41⅗	.892⅖
	Half Dimes	5¢	18 9/16	20⅘	.892⅖
Copper	Cent	1¢	264	264	1.000
	Half Cent	½¢	132	132	1.000

Note: This table applies only to the first coinage specified by the Act of April 2, 1792. Changes in weight and fineness are noted under each coin in Chapter VI.

The First Coinage Act Concluded

Section 10

"And be it further enacted, That upon the said coins respectively, there shall be the following devices and legends, namely: Upon one side of each of the said coins there shall be an impression emblematic of Liberty and the year of the coinage; and upon the reverse of each of the gold and silver coins, there shall be the figure or representation of an eagle with this inscription: 'United States of America,' and upon the reverse of each of the copper coins there shall be an inscription which shall express the denomination of the piece, namely, cent or half cent as the case may require."

1794 Half Dime Reverse

While the act was very specific regarding the devices, it failed to require the denomination on gold and silver coins.

Half Cent Reverse

The act assumed there would be less difficulty in recognizing the value of gold and silver coinage than there would be with copper pieces.

Reverse of Type 4 1837 Half Dime

The omission of value on all but copper coinage was noted, and corrected in Section 13 of the Act of January 18, 1837. It reads in part: ". . . and upon the reverse of each of the gold and silver coins, there shall be the figure or representation of an eagle with the inscription United States of America, and a designation of the value of the coin, but on the reverse of the dime, half dime, cent and half cent, the figure of the eagle shall be omitted."

Reverse of Type 5 Half Dime

The First Motto

E. PLURIBUS UNUM

This motto, which means "One unity composed of many parts," was considered appropriate by Thomas Jefferson, Benjamin Franklin, and John Adams in their first design of the Great Seal of the United States in 1776.

Although it appeared on our coinage as early as 1797, it was not required by law until Section 13 of the Act of February 12, 1873 was enacted. It read in part the same as previous enactments and provided for the same consideration of devices and inscriptions, but it added the requirement that E PLURIBUS UNUM be inscribed on all coins bearing the figure of an eagle.

The same section suggested the use of the motto IN GOD WE TRUST as optional. It read ". . . the Director of the Mint, with the approval of the Secretary of the Treasury, may cause the motto 'In God We Trust' to be inscribed upon such coins as shall admit of such motto."

Obviously, one of the two officers elected to pass that particular option because the motto referred to did not appear on coins until 1864.

Reverse of Half Eagle 1797

The Second Motto

IN GOD WE TRUST

Two Cent Obverse

The option provided by the Act of February 12, 1873, was made mandatory on May 18, 1908, by the following: ". . . be it further enacted, That the motto, 'In God We Trust,' heretofore inscribed on certain denominations of the gold and silver coins of the United States of America, shall hereafter be inscribed on all such gold and silver coins of said denominations as heretofore."

The instructions from Secretary of the Treasury Salmon P. Chase to the director of the mint at Philadelphia on November 30, 1861, had little effect in making the use of this motto mandatory on all coinage of the United States. They read: "No Nation can be strong except in the strength of God, or safe except in His defense. The trust of our people should be declared on our national coins. You will cause a device to be prepared without unnecessary delay with the motto expressing in the fewest words possible the intention suggested."

The motto has not appeared consistently on any series until the cent of 1909, the nickel of 1938, the dime of 1916, the quarter of 1866, the half-dollar of 1866, and the dollar of 1866.

A law passed by the 84th Congress and approved by President Eisenhower on July 11, 1955, ordered that IN GOD WE TRUST must appear on coins and paper currency of the United States. A joint resolution of the 84th Congress and President Eisenhower's approval on July 30, 1956, decreed IN GOD WE TRUST to be the national motto of the United States.

CHAPTER IV

DEVICES, DESIGNS, AND SYMBOLS

A device is a contrivance of one or more symbols that best represent the virtues peculiar to our form of government, each capable of an interpretation not in conflict with the principles of heraldry. It is required by law to occupy either or both sides of a United States coin; separate from, but in conjunction with, inscriptions, mottoes, dates, and denominations also prescribed by the issuing authority.

Until 1909 all U.S. coins bore abstract symbols as main devices on their obverses. In compliance with the provisions of the coinage act, this symbol necessarily represented Liberty, usually in the form of a female bust. Other abstract symbols in use were the shield, the star, and the eagle.

On the death of President Abraham Lincoln, the United States acquired its first specific symbol, but it wasn't until 1909 that his effigy appeared on one of our coins. Mr. Lincoln personified the Four Freedoms; Jefferson and Washington were merely proponents of the Four Freedoms, and their profiles would not have been justified as a symbol of specific value. While placing the likeness of any person on a coin may appear to be a matter of simple mechanics, in actuality a symbol on any coin represents that nation's political ambitions, and their deeds are judged accordingly. For that reason a specific symbol must of necessity be proof of the fulfillment of the political promise made and kept in good faith.

The Phrygian Slave's Cap

There are few symbols on any coinage that can be considered original. Practically all the symbols that appear on coins of the United States, including the Presidential profiles, are facsimiles or abstract conceptions of early Roman symbols. Their perpetuation through the medieval period was due largely to their value as political expedients.

The Phrygian slave's cap, so closely associated with our early coins, is a symbol dating back 2500 years to the Phrygians of Asia Minor. The peaked, rimless headdress was adopted by the Roman freedmen to distinguish themselves from slaves.

In the centuries that followed, this cap symbolized one side or another in revolutionary causes, from the Dutch uprising against Spanish domination through the French Revolution to 1792—the year it was approved as part of a device on the first United States coin issued under the coinage act of April 2, 1792.

The Phrygian cap appears often on coins. Because of special teatment by various designers, the symbol is known numismatically by names other than slave's caps. Those that look more like turbans than peaked caps are called "Turban heads." The device on the dime of 1916 depicts a winged cap, symbolic of "freedom of thought," but the wings gave the cap a new concept that is easier to identify as "Mercury head."

25

Peter the Eagle

The eagle whose likeness appears on most United States coins and paper currency dated after 1855 is officially referred to as "Peter the Mint Bird" in early mint records, and was actually a resident of the Philadelphia mint for a period of six years between the late 1840's and early 1850's. Where he came from or why he chose the pressroom in the mint as his home can only be conjectured, but he did receive special consideration from the mint employees and was permitted to come and go as he pleased.

Peter was exceptionally inquisitive during an actual minting process. He enjoyed watching coining operations and would get as close to the action as possible, remaining there until he was satisfied he had seen all there was to see. This seeming intellectual curiosity on the part of Peter proved to be a key factor in the sudden termination of his career as an observer.

It happened during a test strike of new dies. He became so engrossed in the activities around the large press that he failed to notice a workman starting the press on which he was perched. The sudden lurch of the flywheel threw him to the floor, causing internal injuries that proved fatal despite the care and attention of the crew.

A taxidermist hired by the entire mint personnel repaired Peter's broken wing and mounted him in a glass case in the mint cabinet room. Here he continues to model for his likeness on government obligations. His future as a model for our coinage is assured by the coinage law requiring an eagle on all coins above the denomination of a dime.

The Eagle

Many of our eighteenth-century designers and engravers were Europeans completely unfamiliar with our eagle, which accounts, in part, for the bird's close resemblance to a chicken.

Secondly, devices for that period were engraved directly, with the artist rendering to the die, which is extremely difficult without the aid of a reducing machine.

Nineteenth-century engravers in most instances showed some degree of familiarity with the bald eagle by depicting him as the healthy, sharp, appealing specimen that he really is.

Like many of our symbols, the cagle was a device on early Roman coinage.

That the United States tried desperately to stay clear of the European conflict is reflected in the principal coin designs of 1916. Engravings of the eagle veer from his normal air of defiance to one of sheer peace and tranquillity.

Ornithologists of reputable background consider the eagle on a 1916 quarter dollar a freak, with the head of a hawk, the wings of an eagle, and the body of a dove.

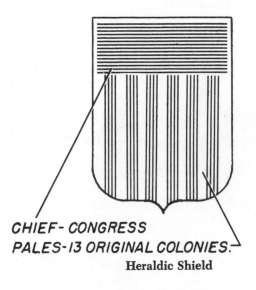

CHIEF- CONGRESS
PALES-13 ORIGINAL COLONIES.

Heraldic Shield

The Shield

The shield is the most centrally located of all symbols in the device, yet it is the one most taken for granted or misunderstood. Actually, the American shield tells more about the United States and its democratic form of government than all the symbols on our currency put together.

In heraldic art the shield surface is called the escutcheon. In most cases it occupies a position of prominence and is usually inscribed with flattering symbols dramatizing the accomplishments of the owner.

To insure accuracy of expression, heraldic engravers used a series of lines and dot patterns to distinguish between colors and metals. Only three of these patterns appear on the American shield. Red, or gules, is indicated by vertical lines; white, or argent, by the absence of a pattern, and blue, or azure, by horizontal lines.

The main features of our shield are the chief, the blue field at the top representing the Congress of the United States, and uniformly spaced vertical lines that represent the thirteen original colonies and the unity that existed among them.

The position of the lines on the shield shows the support of the colonies for Congress. The span of the blue field symbolizes Congress holding the colonies together while completely dependent on their support.

The shield outline binds the states in a mutual defense of a common cause, and its displayed position on the eagle's breast without attachments holding it in place announces to the observer that the United States can rely completely on their own virtues without support.

Accepting the rules of heraldry as a means of identifying the arrangement of stripes, the majority of shields displayed on coins of the United States show seven white and six red stripes. Although the total of thirteen is correct, their positions should be reversed to seven red and six white stripes in keeping with the traditional plan of our national colors.

Four gold coins do show shields of the latter arrangement. They are the Quarter Eagle of 1796, the Half Eagle of 1795 and 1797, and the Eagle of 1797.

A second departure from the rule occurred when Frank Gasparro failed to apply the heraldic pattern for the blue field and red stripes on the reverse of the Kennedy Half-Dollar. This stylized version is a rare application of the shield, relying completely on the ability of the beholder to accept it in its proper prospective.

Exception should not be taken to this practice since there is nothing binding the design of a coin to the principles of heraldry, especially when a deviation from the norm does not affect the interpretation. Attention has been called to the different adaptations purely in the interest of simple translation as it relates to the symbol system in America.

The proper balance between stripe arrangements does not essentially determine the meaning of the shield, nor does its shape or supporting appointments.

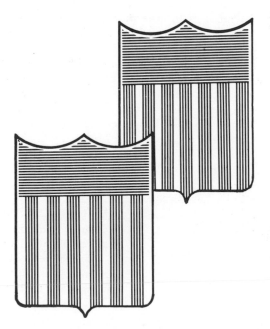

The Star

The five-point star as it appears on our coinage from 1892 to date is a symbol from French heraldry. The six-point star that preceded it on our coinage prior to 1892 is a symbol of English heraldry. In American artistry it is a designative symbol of no interpretable value. Both are early Roman signs, and both have filtered through generations of armorial uses more as appointments than symbols.

A given number of stars on a coin presumably represents the number of states in the union at the time of issue. The addition, however, or omission of a single star is the prerogative of the designer rather than an error in judgment (ref: U.S. Coin No. 98 Type II Gold Half Eagle of 1795). The reverse shows sixteen stars but Tennessee, the sixteenth state to establish statehood, was not officially accepted until June 1, 1796.

An example of the artistic value of a star in an overall design is the single application on the obverse of an 1854 Silver three-cent piece. It substantially occupies the entire area, contributing nothing more than a pedestal for the shield.

Historically, the French five-point star in our flag was influenced by the Washington coat of arms, and there is evidence that someone or some influence was responsible for the perpetual use of the English six-point star on our coinage. Since the stars' heraldic values are practically nonexistent, and there is no traditional reason for using either in our national symbolisms, their appearance on our flag and coinage must be seriously considered to have been a matter of political choice.

Research provides two records of account that support this reasoning. The first favors the five-point star and the second rejects it.

In the first instance, a suggestion for the design of the Great Seal of the United States submitted in 1778 by Lovell of Massachusetts, Scott of Virginia, and Houston of New Jersey contained thirteen five-point stars at twelve o'clock above the main device. The device was rejected except for the thirteen five-point stars, which appear in precisely the same spot on the present seal.

The second instance involved a 1791 pattern one-cent piece submitted to Congress by a private coining firm. All the symbols and their relative positions were accepted and reproduced almost identically on the dollar of 1798, except for the five-point stars. They were replaced with the English six-point variety.

Influence of the Seal

A break in the hundred-year-old tradition of using the English star came when Charles E. Barber designed the Quarter and Half-Dollar of 1892. On these pieces the six-point star still occupied the obverse but thirteen five-point stars dominated the area above the eagle—a design undoubtedly influenced by the Great Seal of the United States.

The Great Seal has never been accurately reproduced on any coinage of the United States although several reverses use the components in the seal.

Wreaths and Sprigs

The leaf or wreath work on a coin is usually an appointment outside of the device and serves to soften the overall design by preventing it from becoming too armorial and unattractive. A wreath can be a single stem formed into a continuous circle with the tip and cut end bound by a ribbon and bow, or it can be depicted as two half-wreaths or branches crossed near the cut end and bound in the same manner.

Wreaths, sprigs, or sprays can be divided into two distinct categories, the foliage and the agricultural.

Foliage is either laurel, oak, palm, or olive, with the latter being the only one of the four with a symbolic value in the Great Seal of the United States: The olive sprig is a Roman symbol of peace. Its irregular leaf pattern distinguishes it from the uniform leaf arrangement of laurel and oak.

The agricultural spray is a combination of colonial America's four major agricultural products—corn, cotton, wheat, and tobacco. No less than two of these products appear in a spray or cluster, with rare exception. The Lincoln Cent reverse shows a pair of long-beard wheat heads flanking the denomination.

Oak

The oak leaf is the least common of the foliage symbols. Two half-wreaths of oak make up the reverse design on the Type III and Type IV Indian Head Cents. A single oak sprig is used with a laurel sprig on the reverse of the Roosevelt Dime.

Palm

A single palm branch and a single laurel branch make up the wreaths on some of the earlier coins.

The single palm branch and a laurel wreath are used in the early dollar reverses, and on some gold pieces.

Arrows

The arrow, both as a weapon and as a symbol, is as ancient an armorial device as any used today, but the arrow on a coin of the United States is typically American Indian in origin. It was a product of real accomplishment and a preference to the designer and engraver.

Symbolically, the arrow is a symbol of war, but as used in the design of a coin, it is toned down to a symbol of preparation. Held in the right talon of the eagle on a crest, it indicates an inclination to be hostile. One or more arrows in the left talon show a readiness for any situation threatening the peace and tranquillity of the owner.

Earlier denominations inadvertently placed the arrows in the right talon, but this was hurriedly corrected before any real significance could be attached to it.

Arrows in Right Talon   **Arrows in Left Talon**

Designers' Signatures

Coinage laws do not require a designer to sign his work nor do they prevent him from doing so. Although his initials are unrelated to the purpose of the design, they may be placed inconspicuously on one or both sides of the coin legally.

Designers' initials as they appear on coinage of the United States are listed here alphabetically together with their work.

Augustus Saint-Gaudens
The initial A embayed by the initial G is below the date on the Standing Liberty Twenty-Dollar gold piece.

Charles E. Barber
The initial B is on the neck truncation of the Barber Head Dime and Quarter Dollar and Half-Dollar of 1892.

Victor D. Brenner
His initials V.D.B. are on the lower reverse rim of the 1909 Lincoln Head Cent and on the sleeve cutoff of cents made since 1918.

John Flanagan
The letters JF are located to the back of the truncation on the Washington Quarter Dollar.

James E. Fraser
The incuse letter F is just below the date on the Indian Head (Buffalo) five-cent piece.

Anthony DeFrancisci
The monogram A over F is just below the neck line of Liberty on the Peace Dollar.

Frank Gasparro
His initials FG are to the right of the shrubbery on the 1959 Memorial Cent reverse; at the apex of the eagle's left leg and the last tail feather on the Kennedy Half-Dollar; under the center tail feather on the Eisenhower Dollar and in the neck truncation of the Eisenhower portrait.

C.Gobrecht F.

Christian Gobrecht
His signature as it appears under the obverse device on the 1836 specimen dollar. F is for *Fecit*—". . . made it."

L

James B. Longacre
The letter L as it appears transverse on the ribbon, partially exposed between the hair and last feather on the Indian Head one-cent piece, and on the neck truncation on his gold coins. Some may show the monogram JBL.

M

Hermon A. MacNeil
The incuse M is to the right of the lowest right-hand star on the obverse of the Standing Liberty Quarter Dollar.

M

George T. Morgan
His initial M is at the tip of the hair scroll on the truncation of the neck and the left loop of the ribbon on reverse of the 1878–1921 Dollar.

B.L.P.

Bela Lyon Pratt
The initials BLP are above the date on the Indian Head Quarter Eagle and Half Eagle.

Gilroy Roberts
His stylized GR is on the truncation of the neck on the Kennedy Half-Dollar.

FS

Felix O. Schlag
The FS is between the coat-sleeve cutoff and the rim on Jefferson Nickels issued since 1966.

JS **JRS**

John R. Sinnock
His JS is on the field, forward of the date and under the neck, on a Roosevelt Dime. His JRS is on the neck truncation on the Franklin Half-Dollar.

Designers' Signatures Concluded

A.A. Weinman
His monogram A under A over W on the Walking Liberty Half-Dollar is to the right of the ledge under the eagle's tail feathers. The monogram A under W is between the rim and base of the neck on a Mercury Dime.

United States Mint Marks

A mint mark is usually the first letter in the name of the city in which the minting facility is located. It is an identification for the control of quality and production, and is not related to the purpose of the design.

From 1942 to 1945, a mint letter appeared on products of the Philadelphia Mint. After the introduction of clad coinage (sandwich coins with a copper center) in 1965, however, mint letters were discontinued on all coins. The practice was resumed in 1968.

P	Philadelphia, Pennsylvania. On wartime silver five-cent pieces only. 1942-1945.
D or **D**	Denver, Colorado—Branch mint. An active facility.
S or **S**	San Francisco, California—Branch mint and U.S. Assay Office. An active facility.
C	Charlotte, North Carolina. Gold only. Discontinued.
CC	Carson City, Nevada. Discontinued.
D	Dahlonega, Georgia. Gold only. Discontinued.
O	New Orleans, Louisiana. Discontinued.

CHAPTER V

HOW UNITED STATES COINS ARE MADE

Early Dies, 1792-1836

Except where Congress determines otherwise, the design on a coin may not be changed more often than once in twenty-five years, from and including the year of the first adoption of the design.

When a design has completed its twenty-five years of service, it may be continued or it may be replaced by an appropriate design selected by the director of the mint with the approval of the Secretary of the Treasury.

Once the motifs have been agreed upon by the principals involved, a series of comprehensive sketches are prepared for both sides of the coin by the chief engraver of the mint and submitted to the director for approval. The final design must lend itself to normal coining practices; special attention is given to the correct curvature of the field and the height of the device.

From 1792 to 1836 all designs were engraved directly onto the face of a master die from the original sketch, which required the drawing to be the exact size of the proposed coin. Master dies were never used for coining, and while the approved sketches may have included all of the symbols for the new design, it isn't likely that the working drawings were any more than a sketch of the central figure with guidelines for supporting appointments.

Design Preparation

When the approval drawings were prepared larger than the actual size of the coin, it was necessary for the artist to reduce each to a working size in direct proportion to that of the original by whatever means he had at his disposal.

Since the transfer process invariably rendered the drawing useless for **additional dies**, the engraver usually prepared a sufficient number of extra copies at the start to insure consistency.

Engraver's Guide

The working drawing usually consisted of the central device, with all details added and indexed as a guide to assure proper balance between the device and whatever symbols were to occupy the area around it.

Inscriptions, stars, and dates were not applied to the master die. They were added to the working die, which accounts for the numerous varieties of one type or denomination.

Die Preparations

Cracked dies were responsible for most of the irregularities in our early coinage. If a die were to survive, even temporarily, it had to be forged from a steel of medium fineness.

Die Sections

Proper die steel must resist hardening under pressure and still withstand the hardening processes without shattering.

When steel of this quality could be found, it was purchased by the mint in random lengths and converted to shorter die sections. The coiner annealed these sections to a working malleability by heating them in a container of hot charcoal and allowing them to cool slowly.

Only those sections completely free of irregularities were selected as die blanks, and each was bathed in a nitric-acid bath to dissolve all small particles of raw iron in the composition, especially around the working area.

Good sections were conically machined at one end to a diameter slightly larger than the finished size of the coin.

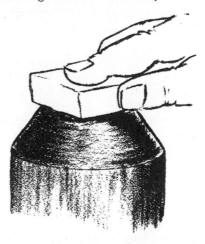

Polished Die

After machining, the blanks were examined for tiny fissures that could create a sizeable problem after the die was made.

The image surface was dressed down with a dead-smooth file and hand lapped with an oil stone to bring the surface to almost a mirror finish.

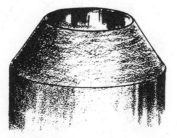

All finished die blanks were transferred from the coining room to the engraver's work area where they became his property until a satisfactory master die had been executed.

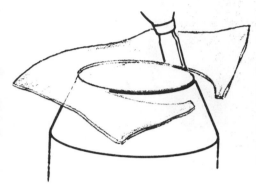

The die blank chosen as the vehicle for the first engraving was cleaned and made ready for a thin layer of transfer wax—a transparent composition in sheet form similiar to heavy tracing vellum.

It was made fast to the face of the die blank with slight hand pressure and the excess was trimmed from the edge of the die face.

Design Laydown

The engraver carefully positioned a copy of the original drawing face down on the wax and centered it within a periphery line of the coin.

An adhesive quality of the wax prevented the tracing from slipping while each line was gently burnished into the wax with a spoon-shaped tool.

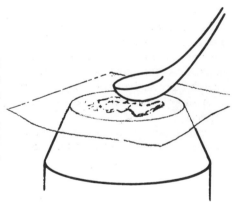

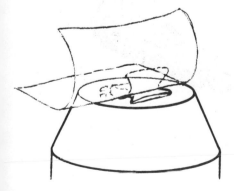

When the engraver felt that the transition was thorough enough, he lifted the tracing in a peeling manner to insure against parting the wax from the face of the die.

Lines important to the general configuration were strengthened and any unnecessary lines were removed or ignored during the engraving process.

Die and Reverse Art

Sinking the design into a die face was not made easier by any mental image the engraver may have had of his original drawing. While engraving he had to think and work in complete reverse. Depth lines in the sketch were now the shallow areas of the cavity, and the shallow areas of the sketch were in fact the deepest impressions in the cavity.

A slip of the chisel or graver (the engraving tool) was not easily rectified, especially toward the end of the job. This may account for variations in certain small details between two coins of the same design. A strand of hair or the trailing end of a ribbon could vary with each die.

Graver

The Basic Gravers

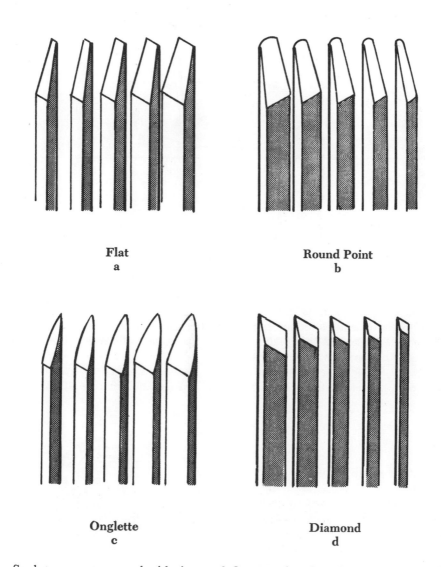

Flat
a

Round Point
b

Onglette
c

Diamond
d

Sculptors, engravers, lapidaries, and fine watchmakers have a variety of special tools with which to pursue their arts. The engraving tool, or graver, as it is commonly referred to, comes in a myriad of shapes and sizes. A basic set will usually consist of (a) the flat, (b) the round point, (c) the onglette, and (d) the diamond. The flat and round gravers are used to remove metal in considerable amounts, while the pointed and diamond shapes are mostly for fine lines.

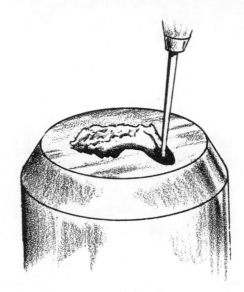

The Master Die

The engraver worked meticulously through the wax, cutting each line into the steel until a major portion of the image took on a recognizable shape. He controlled the quality of his work by periodic impressions of the cavity with a piece of modeling clay.

This was particularly successful when it was necessary to maintain the accuracy in details that could otherwise change the interpretation of the entire device.

A finished die had to be hardened before it could be used in the hubbing operation. It was subjected to the extreme heat-rapid cooling process and then tempered gradually by boiling in a vat of water and cooling slowly.

The master die was now ready to make a first impression—a likeness in reverse as it would appear on a coin. It would be raised on a hub, which in turn would sink a series of working dies, identical to the master.

Hubbing

To assure complete cooperation with the master die, the hub underwent an annealing process to reduce resistance to pressure.

Its machined taper on the service end was identical to the tapered end of the die, except where the die had a flat image area, in which case the hub rose to a coned point.

This provided sufficient metal to properly disperse and fill the die cavity without disturbing the surface below the periphery point.

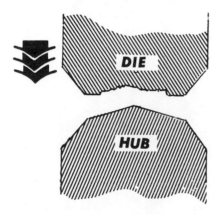

Each time a piece of soft metal is subjected to extreme pressure, it hardens to a dangerous degree and must be re-annealed before the next strike.

The annealed hub was placed in the cup of a multiplying press (screw type) and the inverted master die brought down with enough force to start an impression in the cone.

After each strike it was necessary to draw the hub back to its proper temper.

The process of annealing renders a piece of steel less brittle by heating in a closed pot or oven to prevent oxidation, and allowing it to cool slowly and naturally. Dies and coins must be annealed in order to increase their malleability and insure against cracking and shattering.

Hardening renders firm, or strengthens, a piece of steel that has been annealed or softened by heating it to a cherry-red color and cooling it rapidly in a tank of running water with a rapid motion until the abullition has stopped. Involuntary hardening is brought about by extreme external pressure causing internal stress on the crystal structure. It is actually a natural squeezing-out of fiber imperfections.

Sketch

In Wax

In Steel

On Coin

The Hub

The finished hub gave the engraver his first opportunity to examine it closely and add whatever detail it lacked or lost during the transition. If no further corrections were indicated, it was prepared for the role of a multiple punch. With a coating of linseed oil and lampblack to protect its image, the hub was heated to a brilliant cherry red in a charcoal oven and cooled in a tank of cold water.

This brought the hub up to a dangerously brittle hardness. The face was then polished with an oil and emery compound, and to draw it back to the proper temper, it was heated to a straw-colored glow on an iron bar and allowed to cool slowly.

As the upper stake in a die-stamping press, the hub punched the main device into any number of working dies required for the coining process.

The Working Die

The working die, with just the central device sunk in its surface, was actually a one-to-one copy of the original master die. It was returned to the engraver to be completed, and at this point he was right back where he started—doing everything in reverse. This time, however, he used punches rather than gravers and chisels.

Referring back to the original sketch, the design was completed by punching the stars, inscriptions, and date around the device already sunk by the hub.

Nothing of record indicates the use of an indexing device to locate the position of the appointments in a uniform manner. It was chiefly a matter of skill acquired through trial and error.

While the perfectionist may find it difficult to accept these methods of producing a die, he will have to concede that the end product offered something more than a stamping from a completely mechanized system.

The working die of the first mint resembled pretty much the working die of today. It could be dated and used to strike coins or hub a series to be dated at random.

48

Hand Stamping

Reserving the stamping of symbols and dates for the working die rather than sinking them in the master die was as much a matter of convenience as economy.

Since the main device conformed to law, it wasn't likely to change as often as the date. Secondly, a major mistake in sinking a sign in a working die would not mean the loss of an expensive engraving.

The most logical reason from the very beginning was that mint presses could not distribute an even pressure over the central and peripheral areas of the design.

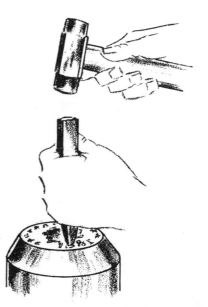

Overdating

A symbol, numeral, or letter not in alignment with the general order of its counterparts, whether double punched or struck over itself or a symbol other than itself, is an error in judgment and not the result of a mechanical malfunction.

Such situations result from the use of a punch to correct an impression and permitting a punch to bounce under a series of rapid blows; or deliberately sinking a letter or numeral over one of a previous mint or date in an effort to destroy the original cavity.

Perfect or imperfect, once a die had been hardened and tempered, it was put into service and allowed to produce undetermined amounts of varieties before it was cancelled and replaced.

Rim Dies

The third die used in the final operation can produce only a plain or reeded edge because the design is consistent with the action of the press.

A coin with this tranverse impression is said to have a milled or reeded edge and the ridges are called "reedings" (or erroneously, "millings").

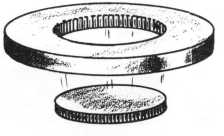

Ornate Rims

Ornate designs were created to discourage "shaving" and were usually applied to gold coins in either relief or incuse.

To remove a coin with an ornate rim from the collar, a multisection die was inserted into a solid outer ring. The pressure of the obverse and reverse dies "squeezed" the edge of the coin planchet into the design.

To remove the coin, it was necessary to "punch out" the entire assembly to allow the multisections to pull away from the components of the design.

In the earlier coinage this was accomplished by striking the coin with a small wood mallet.

This method was later replaced by the Castaing process in which a coin's edge is rolled between two horizontal parallel dies in much the same manner as a pencil is rolled between the fingers.

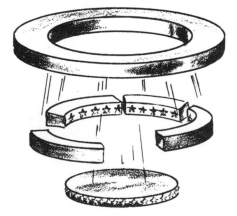

The die-production problem that plagued the mint during its first few years obviously could not continue as a way of operation in our coinage system, and in 1836 the mint adopted the portrait lathe as a mechanical means of producing master dies from original models.

This all but eliminated the need for hand-to-die engraving, and in 1867 the new process was improved with the installation of a Hill reducing machine.

In 1907 this operation was brought to the near peak of efficiency with the Janvier lathe—a highly sensitive pantographic instrument considerably more versatile in transmitting intricate designs.

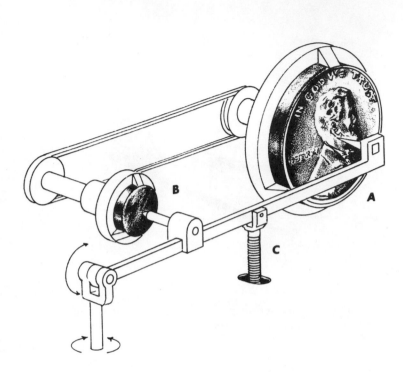

The Janvier Lathe

A pantograph functions on a single plane to accurately reduce or enlarge the details within an area on that plane.

The principle of the Janvier lathe is equivalent to two pantographs working transversely to each other to simultaneously reduce or enlarge the details within an area of their respective planes. Simply stated, it transmits the depressions and elevations of an engraving concurrent with its outline.

Assembled in the lathe, the original model (a) and the steel die blank (b) revolve together at a very low speed. The distance between the two determines the size of the finished die, and for that reason the high-speed cutter on the tracer arm and the die chuck are adjustable.

The attaching control (c) disciplines the vertical movement of the arm while lowering it micrometrically. The sensitivity of this adjustment can increase or decrease the depth of the relief, regardless of the relief on the model.

The Modern Hub

A Janvier lathe produces the hub direct from an artist's model that also includes the legends and date. Only the mint marks are punched into working dies made from the hub.

The tracer point is stationary and centered on the model, while the cutter, rotating at a high rate of speed, is centered on the die face. Both the model and die revolve in a clockwise direction.

During the process the tracer arm moves mechanically downward, passing the tracer point over the relief and transmitting its action through the arm to the cutter and proportionately into the face of the die.

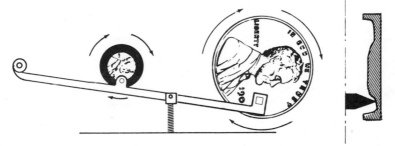

As the cutting progresses, the reduced image begins to appear in the center of the hub.

The normal position of the tracer is against the field or the lowest point in the design. It is raised by the relief and returned by the adjustment controlling the extent of the relief.

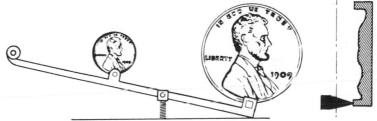

The Kennedy Half-Dollar

February 14, 1967

Dear Mort—

Replying to yours of February 4, the designing of a new coin usually involves the creation of a number of sketches for both sides. However, in the case of the Kennedy Half-Dollar, the motifs to be used were agreed on beforehand by those principally concerned, the secretary of the treasury, director of the mint, Mrs. Kennedy, and perhaps a few others.

Since the time available was so limited, it was necessary that we proceed directly with suitable models, designing and arranging as the work progressed.

Normally, processing a new coin from sketches to finished die takes from two to four months, allowing time for approval of sketches, resolving difficulties, etc. In the case of the Kennedy coin, it was accomplished in about four weeks. Of course, we had a head start not having to make sketches and also being fortunate enough to come up with a piece that apparently pleased all concerned the first time.

Please let me know if I can be of further help.

Cordially yours,
Gilroy Roberts
Former Chief Engraver to the U.S. Mint

The Model

Starting with a sculptured likeness of Mr. Kennedy the engraver had prepared on a previous occasion, he was able to relocate the profile, adjust the curvature of the field, and position the lettering satisfactorily in the first attempt. From here on the process assumes the normal routine.

The Galvano

A mold and positive cast are made from the plastilene model to be prepared as a galvano for the reducing operation.

Galvanos, or metallic models, are used in the Janvier lathe to insure against possible damage from the tracer point and as a means of holding the design firm during the process.

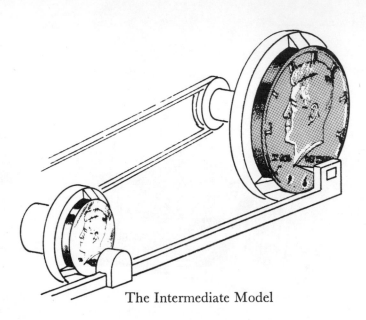

The Intermediate Model

The twelve-inch galvano is placed on the Janvier machine and the design reduced to the surface of a five-inch brass intermediate model. During this operation the relief is partially lowered, leaving the final adjustment to the production of the hub.

When the brass intermediate is completed, it is returned to the engraver for inspection and comparison to the original cast model. Here, details are refined and added that would be much more difficult on the final $1\frac{3}{16}''$ finished hub.

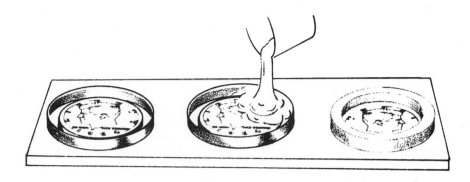

The Hub

All procedures up to this point are repeated once again, only on much smaller pieces. The five-inch brass intermediate is coated with a separating film to prevent possible sticking to the compound, and a mold and positive cast are made just as the original model was made.

The cast is returned to the engravers for final inspection, and any retouching necessary to strengthen the weaker details is performed before submitting it to the director for final approval.

A five-inch galvano of the cast is locked in the Janvier lathe along with a normal die blank. The tracer point and cutter are centered in their respective pieces; instructions to further reduce the relief are fed into the controls and the final result is an impression of the Kennedy Half-Dollar cut into the first hub.

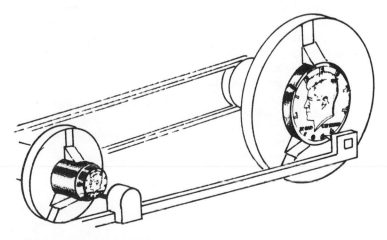

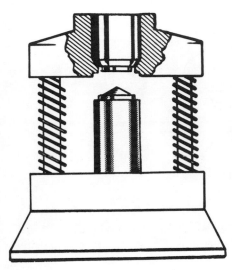

Hubbing

There is no appreciable difference in the hubbing process for the Kennedy Half-Dollar of 1964 and the process used in hubbing the half dollar of 1864, except for the quality of the equipment.

The hub is placed in the head of the holder from the top, and a coned blank die is centered under it on the bed.

A shoulder around the lower edge of the opening prevents the hub from dropping through, and two springs maintain the distance between the hub and blank until they are brought together by pressure.

The entire assembly is centered under the hammer of the multiplying press and subjected to a strike or pressure equivalent to an x number of tons, varying with the size and denomination of the die.

The first strike makes a slight impression on the cone, after which it must be removed and annealed to insure enough malleability for the next strike and a deeper impression.

The ensuing strikes are much the same as the first except when the holder is not used. The hub and die, hand held in the press, are engaged by "feeling" one into the other.

A required number of dies are hubbed during this process.

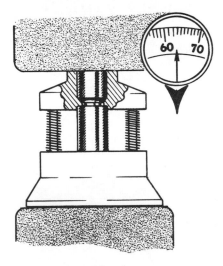

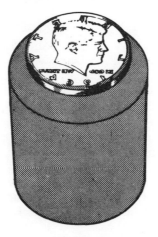

The Working Dies

Each die is examined closely as it comes from the hubbing room and all burrs and rough edges disposed of before it is packed in a charcoal container and subjected to the hardening process. When a die has gone through the extreme heat and rapid cooling cycle, it is too brittle to use as a die and must undergo a medium heat and slow cooling cycle to return to a safe temper.

After a second examination for possible fissures that could develop into a more serious problem, dies that are considered workable are routed to the machine shop to be turned down to fit the multiple die holder during the stamping process.

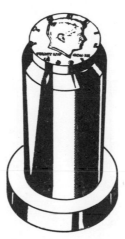

Metals and Alloys

At one time it was necessary for the mint to separate precious metals from whatever alloys and foreign substances with which they may have been mixed. Today the mint limits separating to the mutilated and worn coins returned by the Federal Reserve. Most of the raw pure metal is purchased through competitive bidding from outside sources, and although required to be of a given purity, it is the practice of the mint to insure that purity through tests and refining processes.

The composition of a coin sets down the exact percentage of each alloy in grains. An ingot for the production of a specific coin must contain the alloys proportionate to the coin it will produce. Pure metals have their individual melting points, but a perfect melt is almost guaranteed by alloying at a temperature greater than the melting point, sufficient to provide an even blend.

Table of Melting Points and Densities

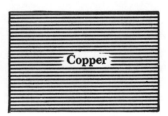

Melting point—1981° F
Density—.323 lbs. per cu. in.
Specific gravity—8.96

Melting point—2646° F
Density—.322 lbs. cu. in.
Specific gravity—8.9

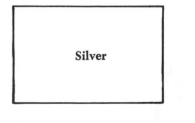

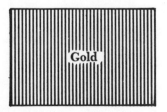

Melting point—1761° F
Density—.380 lbs. per cu. in.
Specific gravity—10.49

Melting point– 1945° F
Density—.697lbs. per cu. in.
Specific gravity—19.32

60

Alloyed Metal

An alloyed melt is a single operation of fusing one or more base metals with a finer metal to form an ingot of specified quality. These ingots, regardless of their composition, are of uniform size to accommodate a standard process of reduction to strips of a precise thickness.

Ingots for the new clad coinage are made by separating two sheets of one metal with a sheet of another and fusing the assembly by detonating an explosive material applied to the outer surfaces.

Ingot Compositions

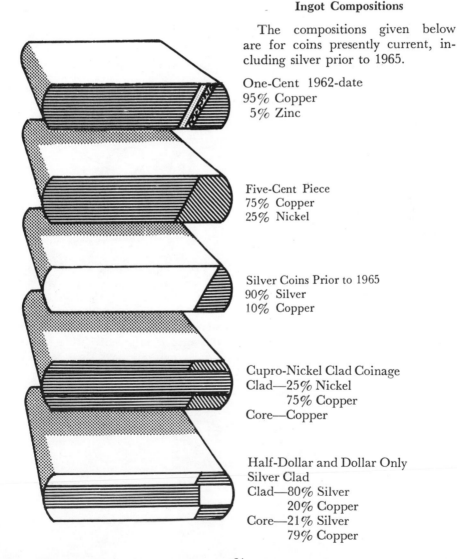

The compositions given below are for coins presently current, including silver prior to 1965.

One-Cent 1962-date
95% Copper
 5% Zinc

Five-Cent Piece
75% Copper
25% Nickel

Silver Coins Prior to 1965
90% Silver
10% Copper

Cupro-Nickel Clad Coinage
Clad—25% Nickel
      75% Copper
Core—Copper

Half-Dollar and Dollar Only
Silver Clad
Clad—80% Silver
      20% Copper
Core—21% Silver
      79% Copper

Rolling

Ingots are molded with a tapered lead end to encourage their first pass through the roller assembly. Scales and burrs that may affect the quality of the planchets are removed with a wire brush, and each ingot is thoroughly cleaned before starting the reduction process.

Blanking

The composition of a strip usually determines the number of passes it must make through the rolling mill to reduce it to a thickness slightly more than that of the finished coin.

A strip is sufficiently wide to provide a minimum of three rows of planchets on a multi-punch press.

Riddle and Polish

It is practically impossible to completely remove all of the residue and particles of metal that attach themselves to a freshly cut planchet.

The larger pieces of scrap are retained at the blanking press, but the payload must undergo a shakedown in the riddle—a sifting action not unlike the old method of separating the wheat from the chaff.

When the blanks leave the riddle, they are polished by tumbling action in a chemical bath.

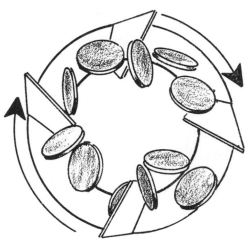

Upsetting

The rim of a coin is its most functional part. It provides a stacking surface and at the same time protects the design on either side against damage from coins it is stacked with. The blank, being slightly larger in diameter than the finished coin, enters the milling machine at a point of its size and rolls through a "passageway" tapered enough to squeeze the excess metal away from the norm at a ninety-degree angle.

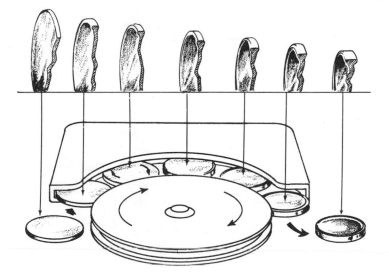

Annealing

At this point the pressures of rolling, blanking, and upsetting have increased the internal stress on the crystal structure of the metal, and the planchets are hardened beyond a workable stage. Before further processing, their tempers must be drawn back to a malleable condition by an annealing period in an open gas-flame furnace.

With the exception of one or two small formalities, the next operation will turn these blanks into finished coins.

Residue from the polishing solution and the film from open gas heat are washed away to insure a perfectly clean planchet for the stamping operation.

Drying

From the washing tumbler, blanks are placed in a revolving drying drum that throws the water off by centrifugal force.

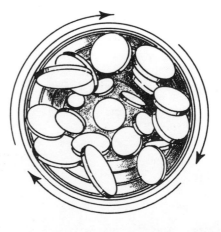

Weighing

Electric weighing devices maintain the accuracy of the blanks and provide a means of checking total weights of the finished coins against those of the ingots addressed to this minting. Silver is weighed twice.

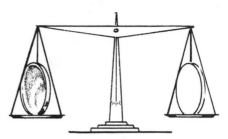

Inspection

Before passing the planchets on to the stamping operation, inspectors examine both sides carefully.

Stamping and Reeding

In one operation and a single stroke, both dies strike impressions on their respective surfaces, and working together, they "squeeze" the edge into the knurling on the reeded collar, and a coin is made.

Tabulation

Newly minted coins are conveyed to a counter where they are bagged and tabulated according to denomination. Each bag identifies the denomination of its contents and the sum total of its value in dollars. The only seal is the stitching to close the bag.

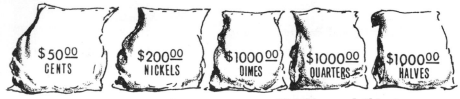

$50⁰⁰ CENTS $200⁰⁰ NICKELS $1000⁰⁰ DIMES $1000⁰⁰ QUARTERS $1000⁰⁰ HALVES

Weighing and Shipping

A second method of checking the bag contents is by weighing. All bags of the announced denomination and value weigh the same. Clad coinage weights of a given denomination are lighter than the same amount of silver coins.

Sealed and weighed bags are shipped via common carrier from the mint to the Federal Reserve Bank.

Distribution

Bagged coins received by the Federal Reserve Bank are opened and counted once again. This is the third checking procedure.

Wrapping

Unless member banks request otherwise, coins are rolled. Additional charges are made for this service, a fourth checking procedure.

Boxing

Rolled coins are prepared for delivery or storage in corrugated and banded cartons. Each carton is marked with the denomination and value, and the name of the distributing authority.

$100⁰⁰	$250⁰⁰	$500⁰⁰	$500⁰⁰
NICKELS	DIMES	QUARTERS	HALVES

National banks are members of the Federal Reserve system and purchase their coinage directly from the district office.

State banks are not members of the Federal Reserve system and must acquire new money through a participating member bank, or through a special membership provided for state banks.

The Coinage Act of 1965

(Modified by the author to express those sections that directly affect the new coinage. All other sections have either been noted elsewhere in the text, or deleted, if not considered useful to the reader.)

Section 1. (a) The Secretary of the Treasury is authorized to cause to be minted and issued the following coins:

(1) A half-dollar or fifty-cent piece, composed of an alloy of eight hundred parts of silver and two hundred parts of copper per each thousand parts by weight, clad on a core of silver-copper alloy so that the composition of each coin shall be four hundred parts of silver and six hundred parts of copper out of each thousand parts by weight

(2) A quarter dollar or twenty-five-cent piece and a dime or ten-cent piece, each composed of an alloy of seventy-five percent copper and twenty-five percent nickel, clad on a core of pure copper.

(b) The cladding alloy used for the outside layers of such coins shall comprise not less than thirty percent of the weight of each coin. Such coins shall be of the same diameter, respectively, as coins of the United States of corresponding denominations at the time of enactment of this act.

Section 2 embodies methods and authorizations for manufacture and designs.

Section 3 establishes legal-tender provisions, to remain current.

Section 4 provides for minting continuance.

Section 5 states that, whenever the Secretary of the Treasury decides action is necessary to protect the coinage of the United States, he is authorized under such rules and regulations as he may prescribe to prohibit the exportation, melting, or treating of coins of the United States.

Section 6 authorizes the sale of excess silver at market price.

Section 7, the purchase of silver at $1.25 per ounce.

Section 8, the acquisition of patents and material.

Section 9, the antidating of coins when necessary.

Section 10, the use of the United States Assay Office at San Francisco as a minting facility on a temporary basis.

Sections 11 through 14 are amendments and clarifications.

Section 15 orders the unobstructed enforcement of this act.

Section 16 establishes a fine or not more than ten thousand dollars or five years imprisonment, or both, for violation of Section 5 on the exportation or melting of any coins of the United States.

Sections 1 through 4 of Title II provide for the appointment, duties, and authority of a Joint Commission on the coinage.

[Shortly before this book went to press, the U. S. Treasury disclosed its intention to request Congress to authorize the production of nonsilver half-dollars and dollars. This move would terminate all silver coinage while restoring those nearly extinct coins to circulation.

Simultaneously the Treasury ended the ban on melting and export of the old silver coins no longer being produced; reduced its weekly sales of surplus silver from 2 million to 1.5 million ounces; and set up an arrangement for the sale of 2.9 million rare silver dollars still reposing in the Treasury's vaults. Meanwhile half-dollars with forty percent silver will continue to be minted at the rate of 100 million pieces annually until Congress approves the recommended legislation. It is expected that the new dollars and half-dollars will be similar in composition to the copper-nickel dimes and quarters.]

The Coinage Act of 1970

Section 201. Section 101 of the Coinage Act of 1965 (31 U.S.C. 391) is amended to read as follows:

Section 101. (a) The Secretary may mint and issue coins of the denominations set forth in subsection (c) in such quantities as he determines to be necessary to meet national needs.

(b) Any coin minted under authority of subsection (a) shall be a clad coin. The cladding shall be an alloy of 75 per centum copper and 25 per centum nickel, and shall weigh not less than 30 per centum of the weight of the whole coin. The core shall be copper.

(c) (1) The dollar shall be 1.500 inches in diameter and weigh 22.68 grams.

(2) The half dollar shall be 1.205 inches in diameter and weigh 11.34 grams.

(3) The quarter dollar shall be 0.955 inches in diameter and weigh 5.67 grams.

(4) The dime shall be 0.705 inches in diameter and weigh 2.268 grams.

(d) Notwithstanding the foregoing, the Secretary is authorized to mint and issue not more than one hundred and fifty million one-dollar pieces which shall have—

(1) a diameter of 1.500 inches;

(2) a cladding of an alloy of eight hundred parts of silver and two hundred parts of copper; and

(3) a core of an alloy of silver and copper such that the whole coin weighs 24.592 grams and contains 9.837 grams of silver and 14.755 grams of copper.

Section 202. For the purposes of this title, the Administrator of General Services shall transfer to the Secretary of the Treasury twenty-five million five hundred thousand fine troy ounces of silver now held in the national stockpile established pursuant to the Strategic and Critical Materials Stock Piling Act (50 U.S.C. 98-98h) which is excess to strategic needs. Such transfer shall be made at the value of $1.292929292 for each fine troy ounce of silver so transferred. Such silver shall be used exclusively to coin one-dollar pieces authorized in section 101(d) of the Coinage Act of 1965, as amended by this Act.

Section 203. The dollars initially minted under authority of section 101 of the Coinage Act of 1965 shall bear the likeness of the late President of the United States, Dwight David Eisenhower.

Section 204. Half dollars, as authorized under section 101 (a) (1) of the Coinage Act of 1965, as in effect prior to the enactment of this Act may, in the discretion of the Secretary of the Treasury, continue to be minted until January 1, 1971.

Section 205 (a) The Secretary of the Treasury is authorized to transfer, as an accountable advance and at their face value, the approximately three million silver dollars now held in the Treasury to the Administrator of General Services. The Administrator is authorized to offer these coins to the public in the manner recommended by the Joint Commission on the Coinage at its meeting on May 12, 1969. The Administrator shall repay the accountable advance in the amount of that face value out of the proceeds of and at the time of the public sale of the silver dollars. Any proceeds received as a result of the public sale in excess of the face value of these coins shall be covered into the Treasury as miscellaneous receipts.

(b) There are authorized to be appropriated, to remain available until expended, such amounts as may be necessary to carry out the purposes of this section.

Section 206. The last sentence of section 3517 of the Revised Statutes, as amended (31 U.S.C. 324), is amended by striking the following: "except that coins produced under authority of sections 101(a)(1), 101(a)(2), and 101(a)(3) of the Coinage Act of 1965 shall not be dated earlier than 1965."

Section 207. Section 4 of the Act of June 24, 1967 (Public Law 90-29; 31 U.S.C. 405a-1 note), is amended by adding at the end thereof the following new sentence: "Out of the proceeds of and at the time of any sale of silver transferred pursuant to this Act, the Treasury Department shall be paid $1.292929292 for each fine troy ounce.

Section 208. Section 3513 of the Revised Statutes (31 U.S.C. 316) and the first section of the Act of February 28, 1878 (20 Stat. 25; 31 U.S.C. 316, 458) are repealed.

Section 209. Coins produced under the authority of section 101(d) of the Coinage Act of 1965, as amended by this Act, shall bear such date as the Secretary of the Treasury determines.

Passed the House of Representatives November 5, 1969.

Passed the Senate with an amendment September 16, 1970.

Proof Coins

Proof coins were originally struck by the mint as cabinet pieces for foreign governments, dignitaries, and museums. Before long, the numismatists were included in this category and eventually sets of proof coins were normal items on the yearly schedule.

These preferred pieces were never struck in excessive quantities until after 1950, but the amount increased rapidly from that year to 1964, when the practice was suspended altogether. Many denominations show no proofs struck during their life span and others show no proofs as a matter of record, although actually some were issued in special situations.

A proof is identical in design to a regular-issue coin except for the sharpness and finish. Because a proof is struck by hydraulic pressure and at a much slower pace than general coinage, its designs and inscriptions are much more defined and similarly higher in relief. The surface is a mirrorlike finish in most cases. Highly polished dies prepare this special finish.

Proof coins are struck from polished perfect planchets (blank metal pieces). They never touch another coin during the process, and with few exceptions, are considered perfect in every way.

When the mint resumed the production of proof coins in 1968, they were struck at the San Francisco facility and bore the mint letter s on the obverse. All previous proofs were the product of the mint at Philadelphia.

Caution: "New Die Proofs" and excellent uncirculated regular-mintage coins have been specially polished and offered as proof coins. These can be detected by examining the letters of the inscription. If they are spread or puffed out, chances are it is not a proof coin. The reedings on the edge will be disturbed and show signs of having been tossed around in shipping. Proof coins, on the other hand, show sharp reedings, sharp and high relief letters, and designs, with more noticeable detail in the hair of the device.

Note: Refer to R. S. Yeoman's *A Guide of United States Coins* for information on Modern Proof Coins and Special Mint Sets.

U.S. Coinage Table of Measurements

Since 1793 the size of all general circulation coinage issued by the United States has been defined by the total number of 1/16th-inch increments in diameter. Mechanically, a ¾" diameter coin was referred to as a Size: 12 because it measured 12/16ths of an inch at its widest point. A 1½" diameter dollar coin was a Size: 24 because the number of 1/16ths of an inch across the center totaled 24.

The following table will determine the size of a coin or medal in millimeters when its exact dimensions are known in inches. There are 16 sixteenths (1/16ths) in one Customary Inch and 25.4 Millimeters in that same inch, referred to here as the "Metric Inch." Thus 16/16ths=25.4 millimeters.

With all U.S. coinage being produced in increments of 1/16th of an inch, it follows that the number of millimeters in one inch, divided by 16, will give the number of millimeters for each 1/16th inch increment, not rounded off to the nearest digit.

Example: 25.4 mm ÷ 16 = 1.5875 millimeters

Starting with the smallest diameter in United States coinage, *U.S. Coin No:* 86 (p.203), the Type I Gold Dollar measures ½ inch, or 8/16ths, across its widest point. This then is a Size 8, or 12.7 millimeters.

Size	8	½"	8/16ths × 1.5875 mm=12.7 mm
	9		9/16ths × 1.5875 mm=14.2875 mm
	10	⅝"	10/16ths × 1.5875 mm=15.875 mm
	11		11/16ths × 1.5875 mm=17.4625 mm
	12	¾"	12/16ths × 1.5875 mm=19.05 mm
	13		13/16ths × 1.5875 mm=20.6375 mm
	14	⅞"	14/16ths × 1.5875 mm=22.225 mm
	15		15/16ths × 1.5875 mm=23.8125 mm
	16	1"	16/16ths × 1.5875 mm=25.4 mm
	17	1 1/16"	17/16ths × 1.5875 mm=26.9875 mm
	18	1 1/8"	18/16ths × 1.5875 mm=28.575 mm
	19	1 3/16"	19/16ths × 1.5875 mm=30.1625 mm
	20	1 1/4"	20/16ths × 1.5875 mm=31.75 mm
	21	1 5/16"	21/16ths × 1.5875 mm=33.3375 mm
	22	1 3/8"	22/16ths × 1.5875 mm=34.925 mm
	23	1 7/16"	23/16ths × 1.5875 mm=36.5125 mm
	24	1 1/2"	24/16ths × 1.5875 mm=38.1 mm
	25	1 9/16"	25/16ths × 1.5875 mm=39.6875 mm

Any variation between these measurements and an accurate micrometer reading may be due to: 1) an under-sized planchet; 2) an over-sized planchet; 3) a worn coin; 4) a shaved coin; or the piece may be counterfeit or altered.

In the event of a conflicting measurement, allow for expansion and contraction of certain metals when held in the hand or when reading is attempted in a room temperature a good deal higher or lower than normal.

PART II

COINOLOGY
1792 to Date

CHAPTER VI

COINAGE OF THE UNITED STATES, 1792 to Date

General Description of Coins

"A Coin *is a piece of metal (gold, silver, copper, etc.) of definite weight and value, usually a circular disc, made into money by being stamped with an officially authorized device.*"

Oxford Universal Dictionary

Coin Components

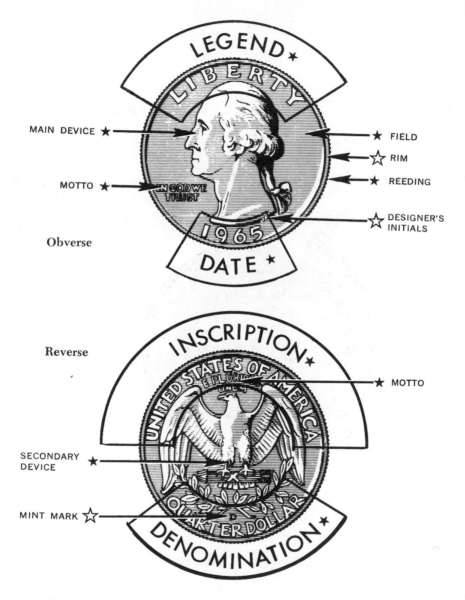

Obverse

Reverse

LEGEND ★

LIBERTY

MAIN DEVICE ★

MOTTO ★

IN GOD WE TRUST

1965

DATE ★

★ FIELD

☆ RIM

★ REEDING

☆ DESIGNER'S INITIALS

INSCRIPTION ★

UNITED STATES OF AMERICA

E PLURIBUS UNUM

★ MOTTO

SECONDARY DEVICE ★

MINT MARK ☆

QUARTER DOLLAR

D

DENOMINATION ★

★ Design properties considered visually essential to an authorized coin of the United States as required by law.

☆ Individual components considered appropriate for their purpose and not necessarily a part of the design. Such symbols are legal but not required by law.

Coin Components

By law each coin of the United States must display certain symbols on its obverse and reverse, and with the exception of the initials of the designer and the mint mark, nothing may be added.

The exact position of each component is controlled only as to which side of the coin it should be applied. Artistic merits are a matter of personal judgment. The eagle must appear on all coins of a denomination larger than ten cents but it is not prohibited on coins of lesser value. The facing direction of the eagle is both a legal and heraldic requirement, but the facing direction of a profile is not.

Coin edges and borders serve as they are designed to without notice except by the most observant professional numismatist or the Secret Service.

Borders are usually nonfunctional designs within the highest point of the rim, and with few exceptions, the pattern is continuous and unbroken. Designs of recent vintage show no borders.

Edges are quite another matter, especially on gold and silver pieces. They are functional, and although they may be treated differently on various occasions, they do safeguard the legal weight and content of the coin. It is one of the oldest deterrents against scraping by those who wish to acquire small portions of gold or silver from several coins without destroying the piece itself.

Except for the twenty-cent piece, all United States silver and gold coins have either a lettered or reeded edge. Earlier half cents, for no particular reason, were occasionally lettered on the edge.

Coin Edges
Ornate, Lettered, and Reeded

	Vine and Bars
E ☆ PLURIBUS ☆ UNUM ☆☆☆☆☆☆☆☆☆☆☆☆	$20.00 Gold
☆☆☆☆☆☆☆☆☆☆☆☆☆☆☆☆☆☆☆☆☆☆☆☆	$10 and $20 Gold
HUNDRED CENTS ONE DOLLAR OR UNIT	Silver Dollars
FIFTY CENTS OR HALF A DOLLAR	Half-Dollars
ONE HUNDRED FOR A DOLLAR	Large Cents
TWO HUNDRED FOR A DOLLAR	Half Cents
	Modern Silver
	Clad

United States Border Patterns

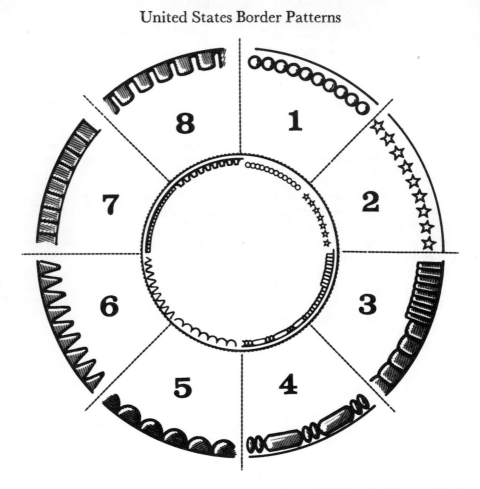

The Lincoln One-Cent Piece, the Indian Head Nickel, the Liberty Head Dime, the Washington Quarter, the Walking Liberty Half-Dollar, and the Peace Dollar were the first coins in their respective denominations to be minted without border patterns. The Standing Liberty Quarter Dollar showed the reel-and-bead design on the obverse but nothing on the reverse.

Border patterns played an important part in earlier designs, but little attention is ever given a border pattern except when it may relate to one of the type variations for a particular denomination.

The U.S. border patterns illustrated are: (1) beaded, (2) starred, (3) denticled, with extremes from short to extended, (4) reel-and-bead, patterned after Roman and Greek architectural designs, (5) engrailed, (6) dancetted (erroneously referred to as serrated), (7) voussoired, meaning a vault curve made round with voussoirs, truncated wedges, (8) embattled denticles, so named because of the early fort embattlements. The valleys are embrasures and the denticles are merlons.

U.S. Coin and Type Series

This section describes the visual and technical properties considered essential to any coin of regular issue authorized by the United States since 1793. It also notes existing unauthorized, altered, and counterfeit pieces by date and description.

The following reference index lists all 119 distinct types of regular-issue coinage in the order of denominational sequence, starting with the half cent through twenty dollars.

"U.S. Coin" number identifies the numerical position of the type in the issue, and "Type" numbers identify its position within a denomination series. The name is a means of distinguishing between designs and may be an official designation, a numismatic classification, or both. The date determines the period in which a type was issued.

Denomination	U.S. Coin	Type	Name	Date	Page
Half Cent	1	I	Liberty Cap*	1793	83
	2	II	Liberty Cap	1794-1797	84
	3	III	Draped Bust	1800-1808	85
	4	IV	Classic Head	1809-1836	86
	5	V	Braided Hair	1840-1857	87
One Cent—large	6	I	Flowing Hair (chain)*	1793	88
	7	II	Flowing Hair (wreath)*	1793	89
	8	III	Liberty Cap	1793-1796	90
	9	IV	Draped Bust	1796-1807	91
	10	V	Classic Head	1808-1814	92
	11	VI	Coronet	1816-1839	93
	12	VII	Braided Hair	1839-1857	94
One Cent—small	13	I	Flying Eagle	1857-1858	95
	14	II	Indian Head*	1859	96
	15	III	Indian Head	1860-1864	97
	16	IV	Indian Head	1864-1909	98
	17	V	Lincoln Head	1909-1942 1946–1958	99
	18	VI	Lincoln Head*	1943	105
	19	VII	Lincoln Head	1944–1945	106
	20	VIII	Lincoln Head	1959 to date	108
Two-Cent Piece	21	I	Shield	1864-1873	110
Three Cents (n)	22	I	Liberty Head	1865-1889	112
Three Cents (s)	23	I	Single-line Star	1851-1853	113
	24	II	Triple-line Star	1854-1858	114
	25	III	Double-line Star	1859-1873	115

U.S. Coin and Type Series Continued

Denomination	U.S. Coin	Type	Name	Date	Page
Five Cents (n)	26	I	Shield—rays	1866-1867	116
	27	II	Shield—no rays	1867-1883	117
	28	III	Liberty Head (wo/c)*	1883	118
	29	IV	Liberty Head (w/c)	1883-1912	119
	30	V	Indian Head (Buf)*	1913	120
	31	VI	Indian Head (Buf)	1913-1938	121
	32	VII	Jefferson Head	1938-1942 1946 to date	123
Five Cents (s)	33	VIII	Jefferson Head	1942-1945	124
Half Dime	34	I	Flowing Hair	1794-1795	130
	35	II	Draped Bust (SE)	1796-1797	131
	36	III	Draped Bust (HE)	1800-1805	132
	37	IV	Liberty Cap	1829-1837	133
	38	V	Liberty Seated	1837-1838	134
	39	VI	Liberty Seated	1838-1860	135
	40	VII	Liberty Seated	1860-1873	137
Dime	41	I	Draped Bust (SE)	1796-1797	138
	42	II	Draped Bust (HE)	1798-1807	139
	43	III	Liberty Cap	1809-1837	140
	44	IV	Liberty Seated	1837-1838	141
	45	V	Liberty Seated	1838-1860	142
	46	VI	Liberty Seated	1860-1891	144
	47	VII	Liberty Head (B)	1892-1916	145
	48	VIII	Liberty Head (M)	1916-1945	146
	49	IX	Roosevelt (s)	1946-1964	148
	50	X	Roosevelt (cl)	1965 to date	149
Twenty Cents	51	I	Liberty Seated	1875-1878	150
Quarter Dollar	52	I	Draped Bust (SE)*	1796	152
	53	II	Draped Bust (HE)	1804-1807	153
	54	III	Liberty Cap (w/m)	1815-1828	154
	55	IV	Liberty Cap (wo/m)	1831-1838	155
	56	V	Liberty Seated	1838-1866	156
	57	VI	Liberty Seated*	1853	157
	58	VII	Liberty Seated	1866-1891	158
	59	VIII	Liberty Head (B)	1892-1916	159
	60	IX	Standing Liberty	1916-1917	160
	61	X	Standing Liberty	1917-1930	161
	62	XI	Washington Head (s)	1932-1964	163
	63	XII	Washington Head (cl)	1965 to date	164

U.S. Coin and Type Series Continued

Denomination	U.S. Coin	Type	Name	Date	Page
Half-Dollar	64	I	Flowing Hair	1794-1795	166
	65	II	Draped Bust (SE)	1796-1797	167
	66	III	Draped Bust (HE)	1801-1806	168
	67	IV	Liberty Cap	1807-1836	169
	68	V	Liberty Cap	1836-1837	170
	69	VI	Liberty Cap	1838-1839	171
	70	VII	Liberty Seated	1839-1866	172
	71	VIII	Liberty Seated *	1853	173
	72	IX	Liberty Seated	1866-1891	174
	73	X·	Liberty Head (B)	1892-1915	175
	74	XI	Walking Liberty	1916-1947	176
	75	XII	Franklin Head	1948-1963	178
	76	XIII	Kennedy Head (s)*	1964	180
	77	XIV	Kennedy Head (scl)	1965–1970	182
	117	XV	Kennedy Head (cl)	1971 to date	184
One Dollar	78	I	Flowing Hair	1794-1795	186
	79	II	Draped Bust (SE)	1795-1798	187
	80	III	Draped Bust (HE)	1798-1803	188
	81	IV	Liberty Seated	1840-1866	191
	82	V	Liberty Seated	1866-1873	192
	83	VI	Trade Dollar	1873-1885	193
	84	VII	Liberty Head (M)	1878-1904, 1921	194
	85	VIII	Liberty Head (Peace)	1921-1935	196
	118	IX	Eisenhower Head (scl)	1971 to date	198
	119	X	Eisenhower Head (cl)	1971 to date	199
One Dollar	86	I	Liberty Head	1849-1854	203
	87	II	Indian Head (f)	1854-1856	204
	88	III	Indian Head (f)	1856-1889	205
Quarter Eagle ($2.50)	89	I	Liberty Cap (wo/s)*	1796	206
	90	II	Liberty Cap (w/s)	1796-1807	207
	91	III	Liberty Cap—Bust *	1808	208
	92	IV	Liberty Cap—Bust	1821-1834	209
	93	V	Classic Head	1834-1839	210
	94	VI	Coronet	1840-1907	211
	95	VII	Indian Head (m)	1908-1929	212
Three Dollars	96	I	Indian Head (f)	1854-1889	213
Half Eagle ($5)	97	I	Liberty Cap (SE)	1795-1796	214
	98	II	Liberty Cap (HE)	1795-1807	215
	99	III	Liberty Cap	1807-1812	216
	100	IV	Liberty Cap	1813-1834	217
	101	V	Classic Head	1834-1838	218

Denomination	U.S. Coin	Type	Name	Date	Page
	102	VI	Coronet (wo/m)	1839-1866	219
	103	VII	Coronet (w/m)	1866-1908	220
	104	VIII	Indian Head (m)	1908-1929	221
Eagle	105	I	Liberty Cap (SE)	1795-1797	222
($10)	106	II	Liberty Cap (HE)	1797-1804	223
	107	III	Coronet (wo/m)	1838-1866	224
	108	IV	Coronet (w/m)	1866-1907	225
	109	V	Indian Head (wo/m)	1907-1908	226
	110	VI	Indian Head (w/m)	1908-1933	227
Double Eagle	111	I	Coronet (wo/m)	1849-1866	228
($20)	112	II	Coronet (w/m)	1866-1876	229
	113	III	Coronet—Dollars	1877-1907	230
	114	IV	Liberty Standing (r/n) *	1907	231
	115	V	Liberty Standing (a/n)	1907-1908	232
	116	VI	Liberty Standing (w/m)	1908-1933	233

* Issued one year only; SE Small Eagle; HE Heraldic Eagle; (B) Barber; (M) Morgan; (s) Silver; (Scl) Silver clad; (n) Nickel; (c) Copper; (cl) clad; (w/m) With Motto; (wo/m) Without Motto; (w/c) With Cents; (wo/c) Without Cents; (f) Female; (m) Male; (rn) Roman Numeral; (an) Arabic Numeral.

Type vs Variety

In the opinion of the author, a legal Type occurs when a major noticeable change is deliberately made in either the physical, metallurgical or design structure of a lawful coin.

On the other hand, any attempt to correct a poorly executed die or an imperfect mechanical operation can create several varieties of a single type.

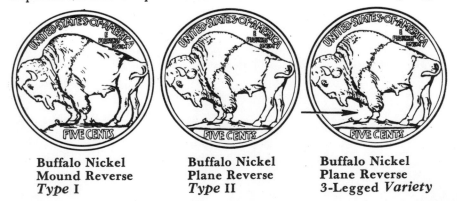

Buffalo Nickel
Mound Reverse
Type I

Buffalo Nickel
Plane Reverse
Type II

Buffalo Nickel
Plane Reverse
3-Legged *Variety*

HALF CENT (LIBERTY CAP), 1793

Specifics

U.S. Coin No.: 1
Type: I Half Cent
Size: 14 or 7/8″
Weight: 104 grains
Edge: Lettered

Composition: Copper
Quantity minted: 31,939
Proofs minted: None of record
Mint marks: None
Designer: Joseph Wright

Description

Obverse: The main device is a female head representing Liberty facing left, with unruly shoulder-length hair held in place at the forehead by a fillet, or band. A pole, topped by the Phrygian slave's cap, over her right shoulder extends from the tip of the neck truncation beyond the back of the head. The inscription LIBERTY is positioned radially above the head, and the date, radially below the neck. A beaded border encloses the field. There are no further markings on the surface.

Reverse: Two curved stems of multi-berried laurel, crossed and tied with a ribbon and single bow, form a wreath around the words HALF CENT. The inscription UNITED STATES OF AMERICA occupies the area around the wreath and the fraction 1/200 is set below. The border is beaded.

Edge: The lettered edge reads TWO HUNDRED FOR A DOLLAR.

HALF CENT (LIBERTY CAP), 1794-1797

Specifics

U.S. Coin No: 2
Type: II Half Cent
Size: 14 or ⅞″
Weight: 104 grains, 1794-95
    84 grains, 1796-97
Edge: 1794-95-97, lettered and
    plain; 1796, plain only

Composition: Copper
Quantity minted: 329,728
Proofs minted: None of record
Mint marks: None
Designers:
    1794, Robert Scot
    1796, John Smith Gardner

Description

Obverse: The main device is the Liberty head facing right. No fillet confines the hair, less unruly than her predecessor's. The pole over the left shoulder holds a more discernible Phrygian cap. Varieties for the year 1795 and 1796 show no pole below the neck area, and one additional variety of the 1795 coin has a punctuation mark after the figure "1" in the date. LIBERTY and the date are in a radius area above and below the device. A series of radial markings form the border.

Reverse: Two half-wreaths of laurel, with fewer berries and a radical leaf pattern, crossed and tied by a ribbon and double bow, are the only difference between the reverses of Types I and II.

Edge: Plain, or lettered to read TWO HUNDRED FOR A DOLLAR.

HALF CENT (DRAPED BUST), 1800-1808

Specifics

U.S. Coin No: 3
Type: III Half Cent
Size: 14 or ⅞"
Weight: 84 grains
Edge: Plain*

Composition: Copper
Quantity minted: 3,425,572
Proofs minted: None of record
Mint marks: None
Designers: Gilbert Stuart
Robert Scot

Description

Obverse: A new interpretation of the Liberty goddess faces right with tresses extending below the shoulder line and partially secured at the back of the head by a ribbon. The draped-bust profile is completely devoid of any symbol, such as the pole and Phrygian slave's cap, to identify her as Liberty. An inscription LIBERTY and the date still appear above and below the device, but are situated much closer to the radial markings of the border.

Reverse: The motifs on Types I, II, and III are basically the same, with the differences caused more by the latitude in design rather than intent. A bolder wreath appears on issues after 1802, and varieties of 1804, 1805, and 1806 show no stems below the ribbon.

HALF CENT (CLASSIC HEAD), 1809-1836

Specifics

U.S. Coin No: 4
Type: IV Half Cent
Size: 14 or 7/8″
Weight: 84 grains
Edge: Plain

Composition: Copper
Quantity minted: 3,637,912
Proofs minted: 6,590,000 from 1831
Mint marks: None
Designer: John Reich

Description

Obverse: A radical departure from all previous designs. The matronly portrait of Liberty faces left. An overabundance of tresses is secured by a headband inscribed LIBERTY. Thirteen six-point English heraldry stars have been added to the field to represent the thirteen original colonies—seven on a vertical radius to the left of the device, and six in a similar position to the right. One variety of the 1828 issue shows only five stars to the right. The date is in exergue, close to the border pattern.

Reverse: The primary motif has been upgraded by a new application of the wreath. A single branch of laurel encircles the words HALF CENT clockwise, with the tip secured to the lower stem by a ribbon and single bow. The clustered leaves are close to the stem. The issuing authority UNITED STATES OF AMERICA almost encompasses the wreath. The fraction "1/200" is omitted.

HALF CENT (BRAIDED HAIR), 1840-1857

Specifics

U.S. Coin No: 5
Type: V Half Cent
Size: 14 or ⅞″
Weight: 84 grains
Edge: Plain

Composition: Copper
Quantity minted: 544,510
Proofs minted: 1840–49 and 1854–57
Mint marks: None
Designer: Christian Gobrecht

Description

Obverse: A profile of definite Roman character is the fourth approach to a device acceptable as symbolic of Liberty. The head, which faces left, is adorned with a coronet, and two strands of beads secure the hair, fashioned into a double bun at the back. Some loose tresses fall to the shoulder area and scrolls under the truncation of the neck. The word LIBERTY is inscribed on the coronet and a circle of thirteen small six-point stars completely involve the field except for the date in exergue.

Reverse: The denticle pattern of the border is well within the periphery of the coin although it reduces the size of the reverse design, which is essentially the same as Type IV.

Edge: Pieces are known to exist with lettered or patterned edges but all are products of a facility outside the mint and unauthorized.

ONE CENT LARGE (FLOWING HAIR/CHAIN REVERSE), 1793

Specifics

U.S. Coin No.: 6
Type: I Large Cent
Size: 17 or 1¹⁄₁₆″
Weight: 208 grains
Edge: Vine and bars

Composition: Copper
Quantity minted: 36,103
Proofs minted: None of record
Mint marks: None
Designer: Henry Voight

Description

Obverse: The "wild" Flowing Hair Liberty facing right on the first large cent was hardly popular with the public, but it is typical of the lack of control an engraver has over working directly into a die. The word LIBERTY and the date are all that are proper in this design. The field is void of further markings and no border is indicated.

Reverse: A chain circle of fifteen links surrounds the denomination ONE CENT and the fractional expression ¹⁄₁₀₀. The inscription UNITED STATES OF AMERICA forms an unbroken pattern around the edge of the field. No border is indicated. One variety of the Type I LARGE CENT omits the letters CA in AMERICA.

ONE CENT LARGE (FLOWING HAIR/WREATH REVERSE), 1793

Specifics

U.S. Coin No: 7
Type: II Large Cent
Size: 17 or 1¹⁄₁₆″
Weight: 208 grains
Edge: Vine and bars; lettered

Composition: Copper
Quantity minted: 63,353
Proofs minted: None of record
Mint marks: None
Designer: Adam Eckfeldt

Description

Obverse: The visual effect of the device on Type II was approximately that of the device on Type I. The hair is unruly but a bit more refined. Because the device is slightly larger, the legend LIBERTY is crowded between the head and the beaded border. A three-leaf sprig of laurel separates the date from the truncation of the neck. One rare variety refers to this sprig as the strawberry leaf, so similar is it to the leaves of that plant.

Reverse: Public rejection of the Chain Reverse is responsible for a multi-berried laurel wreath not unlike that of the Type I Half Cent, which is also tied with a single bow. The denomination ONE CENT appears inside the wreath and the fraction ¹⁄₁₀₀ is below. The border is beaded.

Edge: There are three varieties of the edge: (1) vine and bars; (2) lettered edge with one leaf; and (3) lettered edge with a double leaf. Lettered edges read ONE HUNDRED FOR A DOLLAR.

ONE CENT LARGE (LIBERTY CAP), 1793-1796

Specifics

U.S. Coin No: 8
Type: III Large Cent
Size: 18 or 1⅛″
Weight: 208 grains, 1793-94-95;
    168 grains, 1796
Edge: Lettered and plain

Composition: Copper
Quantity minted: 1,577,902
Proofs minted: None of record
Mint marks: None
Designer: Joseph Wright

Description

Obverse: An attractive head of Liberty faces right with the fall of hair extending below the shoulder line. The pole over her left shoulder is topped by the familiar Phrygian slave's cap. LIBERTY and the date are in radius above and below the head and neck. The border is beaded.

Reverse: Variations of the wreath are almost as numerous as the many other variations in this issue. They are all two laurel branches formed around the denomination ONE CENT and tied by a ribbon and double bow. The ONE CENT may be high in the wreath, or it may center. The inscription of the issuing authority, UNITED STATES OF AMERICA, and the fraction ¹⁄₁₀₀ complete the design. The border may be beaded or denticled.

Edge: Lettered edges read ONE HUNDRED FOR A DOLLAR. Some varieties of the 1795 issue have plain edges. The 1795 reeded edge is rare.

ONE CENT LARGE (DRAPED BUST), 1796-1807

Specifics

U.S. Coin No: 9
Type: IV Large cent
Size: 18 or 1⅛"
Weight: 168 grains
Edge: Plain

Composition: Copper
Quantity minted: 16,009,810
Proofs minted: None of record
Mint marks: None
Designers: Robert Scot
Gilbert Stuart

Description

Obverse: Although the Type III Half Cent and the Type IV Large Cent were not issued simultaneously, they are, nevertheless, companion pieces. Liberty is introduced as a female head without further identification of her role. Strands of the hair, which falls below the shoulder line, are gathered to the back of the head and secured by a multi-bowed ribbon and knot. The required inscription, LIBERTY, and the date curve. The border of the coin is denticled.

Reverse: The general motif is identical to preceding reverses with one noticeable exception: The size of the lettering in UNITED STATES OF AMERICA varies throughout the series.

91

ONE CENT LARGE (CLASSIC HEAD), 1808-1814

Specifics

U.S. Coin No: 10
Type: V Large Cent
Size: 18 or 1⅛″
Weight: 168 grains
Edge: Plain

Composition: Copper
Quantity minted: 4,850,722
Proofs minted: None of record
Mint Marks: None
Designer: John Reich

Description

Obverse: A companion piece to the Half Cent, the design of the Large Cent of 1808 was identical, except that it was slightly smaller. The likeness of Liberty faces left, her excessive hairdo restrained by a headband inscribed LIBERTY and secured at the back of the head with a ribbon. The main device is flanked by seven six-point stars on the left and six on the right, and the date is in exergue below the bust line. One variety of the 1808 issue shows the omission of one star on the lower left, caused by a die break.

Reverse: The inscription UNITED STATES OF AMERICA all but encircles the single-branch laurel wreath bound by a ribbon and single bow. ONE CENT occupies the area within the wreath and is underscored with a line the length of the EN in CENTS. The fractional denomination is omitted.

Unusually large denticles form the border for both sides.

Edge: The edge should be plain. The softness of the metal, however, offered little resistance to marks and indentations that may appear intentional.

ONE CENT LARGE (CORONET), 1816-1839

Specifics

U.S. Coin No: 11
Type: VI Large Cent
Size: 18 or 1⅛″
Weight: 168 grains
Edge: Plain

Composition: Copper
Quantity minted: 56,384,561
Proofs minted: None of record
Mint marks: None
Designers: Robert Scot
William Kneass

Description

Obverse: The less-than-pleasing head of Liberty facing left has a lower hairdo drawn to a double bun at the back and secured by a cord. Her tresses extend below the truncation of the neck and scroll toward the date. A tiara or coronet inscribed with LIBERTY replaces the headband on Type V. Thirteen six-point stars, uniformly arranged around the device, are intergraved at the bottom by the date. The border is a coarse denticle pattern at the extreme edge of the coin.

In this series the date creates the greater number of varieties. It is consistently irregular in spacing, and shows overdating for practically every year of issue, up to 1827.

Reverse: Essentially the same format as previous reverses with one branch of laurel forming a wreath clockwise about the denomination ONE CENT. Two type sizes in the denomination and the inscription UNITED STATES OF AMERICA factor in two varieties for each of the years between 1829 and 1833.

ONE CENT LARGE (BRAIDED HAIR), 1839-1857

Specifics

U.S. Coin No: 12
Type: VII Large Cent
Size: 18 or 1⅛″
Weight: 168 grains
Edge: Plain

Composition: Copper
Quantity minted: 70,918,871
Proofs minted: None of record
Mint marks: None
Designer: William Kneass

Description

Obverse: There is very little difference between the portrait of Liberty on this coin and the portrait on the preceeding Type VI. The coronet is more prominent and the head inclines forward as if in motion, while the Type VI is stout and less forceful. A double strand of beads holds the hair in a double bun, which gives the appearance of braiding. The most noticeable difference between Type VI and VII is the treatment of the hair scroll at the base of the neck. This coin shows a continuation forward while the previous type extends downward.

The date separates a circle of thirteen six-point stars inside the border pattern. Variations in the style and size of the date exist for practically every year of issue.

Reverse: Identical to previous types except that the design is reduced as the space between the border and edge is increased.

ONE CENT SMALL (FLYING EAGLE), (1856) 1857-1858

Specifics

U.S. Coin No: 13
Type: I Small Cent
Size: 12 or ¾"
Weight: 72 grains
Edge: Plain

Composition: 88% copper, 12% nickel
Quantity minted: 42,050,000
Proofs minted: (approx.) 280 rare
(approx.) 1000 in 1856*
Mint marks: None
Designer: James Longacre

Description

Obverse: The eagle (volant) in free flight to the left is in keeping with the legal requirements that a U.S. coin bear an impression emblematic of liberty. At three points—the beak, the right-wing tip, and the tip of the tail feather —the eagle all but touches the denticles in the border design. An inscription of the issuing authority, UNITED STATES OF AMERICA, circumscribes the device from the beak to the tail, and the date is in radius at the base of the field. Two varieties were created by (1) a normal separation between the serifs on A and M in AMERICA, and (2) a continuous serif connecting these two letters.

Reverse: A wreath of corn, cotton, wheat, and tobacco—the four major agricultural products of the United States—envelops the denomination ONE CENT. It was determined that the popularity of the new cent would serve to promote the export commodities of America.

*Some are known as restrikes.

95

ONE CENT SMALL (INDIAN HEAD), 1859

Specifics

U.S. Coin No: 14	*Composition:* 88% copper, 12%
Type: II Small Cent	nickel
Size: 12 or ¾″	*Quantity minted:* 36,400,000
Weight: 72 grains	*Proofs minted:* Unknown
Edge: Plain	*Mint marks:* None
	Designer: James Longacre

Description

Obverse: A simulated head of an Indian girl, facing left, is identified as Liberty by the legend of her headdress. Her shoulder-length hair sweeps back and down to a scroll just under the truncation of the neck.

Her features are accentuated by a highly detailed feather headdress secured by a ribbon with one dovetailed end extending over and forward. It is marked vertically by four diamonds end to end. The opposite end of the ribbon is partially exposed between the hair and last feather. A strand of seven beads lie on the pedestal of the neck.

The inscription UNITED STATES OF AMERICA flanks the device on the left and on the right and the date is radius in the base.

Reverse: Two branches of laurel tied with a ribbon and single bow form a wreath around the denomination ONE CENT. The foliage of the laurel branches is unusually heavy and shows the leaves in uniform clusters.

ONE CENT SMALL (INDIAN HEAD), 1860-1864

Specifics

U.S. Coin No: 15
Type: III Small Cent
Size: 12 or ¾"
Weight: 72 grains
Edge: Plain

Composition: 88% copper, 12% nickel
Quantity minted: 122,321,000
Proofs minted: 3,310
Mint marks: None
Designer: James Longacre

Description

Reverse Changed: Only the reverse design of the "white" cent changed. The wreath of laurel was replaced by wreath of oak, separated at the top by a shield. A ribbon and single bow secure the oak branches

and three arrows pointing to the right.

James Barton Longacre designed the Indian Head device using his daughter Sarah as his model. He was impressed by the idea that a feathered headdress was as typically American as the turban was typically Asian.

He considered it more appropriate as a symbol on our coinage than the Phrygian slave's cap. "We have only to determine that it *shall* be appropriate and all the world cannot wrest it from us." *James B. Longacre*

ONE CENT SMALL (INDIAN HEAD), 1864-1909

Specifics

U.S. Coin No: 16
Type: IV Small Cent
Size: 12 or ¾″
Weight: 48 grains
Edge: Plain

Composition: 95% copper, 5% tin/zinc
Quantity minted: 1,690,916,000
Proofs minted: 96,848
Mint marks: S-1908-09 only
Designer: James Longacre

Description

Obverse: The dark bronze cent was a rarity the first year of its issue. A few of the last coins struck in 1864 carried the initial "L" for Longacre, the designer, in the obverse device, as did all Indian Heads until discontinuation in 1909.

The letter ʟ is fixed tranversely to its normal upright position. It is located on the partially hidden end of ribbon between the hair and the last feather. Place the coin in a readable position and turn a quarter counterclockwise. The ʟ should appear upright, as illustrated.

ONE CENT, SMALL, (LINCOLN HEAD), 1909-1942, 1946-1958

Specifics

U.S. Coin No: 17
Type: V Small Cent
Size: 12 or ¾"
Weight: 48 grains
Edge: Plain

Composition: 95% copper, 5% tin/zinc
Quantity minted: 21,063,560,620
Proofs minted: 3,851,763
Mint marks: D and S
Designer: Victor D. Brenner

Description

Obverse: The main device is a specific symbol of Liberty. The bust of Abraham Lincoln, facing right, extends vertically from just inside the lower rim to the letter line of the motto IN GOD WE TRUST, positioned radially inside the upper rim. It separates the legend LIBERTY on the left from the date on the right. There is no border pattern.

Reverse: Two curved, stylized heads of long-beard wheat flank the denomination ONE CENT over the inscription UNITED STATES OF AMERICA. The motto E PLURIBUS UNUM is positioned radially just inside the upper rim.

The designer's initials, V.D.B., appear against the reverse lower rim, between the stems of the heads of wheat. They were removed the same year.

Note: Various situations involving the design and production of this coin created numerous scarce and rare dates that made it possible to market certain unauthorized pieces. Each of these is illustrated and dealt with individually for the reader's early detection. Any coin of high value considered genuine should still be authenticated before you change ownership.

The Model

Victor Brenner was a great admirer of Mr. Lincoln and often sculpted mementos of his likeness for close friends and associates. One such work is the famous Lincoln plaque, which eventually became the prototype for the One-Cent profile.

President Theodore Roosevelt was shown the plaque during a visit to Brenner's studio to discuss a design for the Panama Canal medal. He was so impressed with the strength of character the features portrayed that he requested Brenner to design a new one-cent coin, suitable to commemorate the hundredth anniversary of Lincoln's birth.

Brenner had placed his name in full on the obverse design in the first set of models submitted for approval. This was rejected and the second set carried only v.d.b. against the reverse lower rim between the wheat-head stems. Secretary of the Treasury MacVeigh objected to three initials on the coin, but 27 million pieces had already been struck at Philadelphia and close to a half-million minted at San Francisco. The initials were removed, however, before the remainder of a year's mintage was completed.

Victor D. Brenner's initials as they appear on the reverse of the 1909 coins minted at Philadelphia and San Francisco.

The reverse of all Lincoln One-Cent Pieces after the initials were removed in 1909.

The 1909-S V.D.B.

While mint marks may vary in their location on many coins of the United States, the Lincoln Cent entitled to a mint mark will always show either D or S just under the center of the date.

The fourth-highest-value Lincoln One-Cent piece is the 1909-S V.D.B. with a total mintage figure of only 484,000 pieces, which makes it rare. A rare coin is always subject to duplication.

A genuine 1909-S V.D.B. Lincoln One-Cent Piece will show the V.D.B. on the reverse—plainly detailed. The initials should still be apparent on badly worn pieces.

Unauthorized coins: It is not impossible to raise the initials V.D.B. on the rim of a 1909-S plain cent issued after the initials had been officially removed. Close examination will expose this "addition." A second method of faking is just as detectable. The letter S has been "lifted" from a common date and "laid" on the field of a 1909 V.D.B. Inspection under a microscope will readily reveal this technique. The third and most recent "fake" discovery is recorded by the American Numismatic Authentication Trust. It is a die struck 1909-S V.D.B. and produced in quantity in southern Europe.

Caution: A legitimate dealer will not offer a high-value coin for sale without first having it authenticated. The demand for rare and scarce pieces is too great to warrant bargain or special prices. Any such offer should be noted unless authenticity is established by a recognized numismatic expert.

The 1914-D

Probably the one coin that has suffered more indignities because of its rarity than any other piece in the entire Lincoln Head series, is the 1914-D Cent.

There were 1,193,000 coins of this date struck at the United States Mint in Denver, the lowest mintage since the 1909-S and the third lowest to date. It is, therefore, a key coin to a numismatist and a piece that is easily marketed without too much sales resistance.

The mint letter D on a genuine 1914-D will be located lower than the D on an altered coin and it is in a much smaller type. If the letter appears in any other position than shown, the coin has undoubtedly been altered.

The 1914-D Altered Date

Any coin bearing a date ending with the figure "4" and a mint letter D can be, and has been, altered to 1914-D.

The most popular date adaptable to this process is the 1944-D. It offers every possibility and very little ingenuity is required by the operator.

Authenticating a 1914-D

This coin requires more than a single process to determine its authenticity. A 1914-D can be altered from a Denver coin of another date; it can be altered from a 1914-S; it can be altered by applying the correct mint letter to a 1914 or to an adjusted "fake"; or, it can be constructed by means of a number of these methods combined.

Genuine   **Fake**

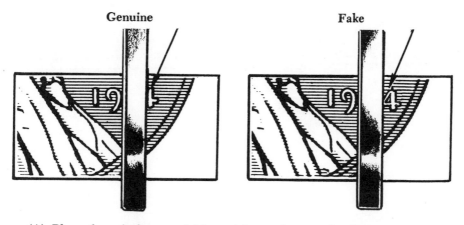

(1) Place the coin in a readable position and cover the figure "1" between the "9" and the "4" with the edge of a second cent held vertically. Allow the second coin to touch but not overlap the trailing edge of the figure "9" on the left. On the right, a genuine 1914-D will show only the vertical bar and crosslet extention of the "4." If any portion of the crosslet shows between the coin you are holding and the bar of the "4," it is undoubtedly an altered 1944-D.

(2) Examine the mint letter D with a magnifying glass, regardless of its position. If it is black around the edge and the surface area appears dark as if burned or overheated, the letter has more than likely been "sweated" on. This applies also to the "1" and the "4" in the date. They could and have been moved closer together by "lifting" and "sweating."

(3) If the date measures out correctly, check the mint letter again. It could have been "chased" from the s on a 1914-S—an easy job for an expert metalsmith, but one that can usually be detected.

(4) The designer's initials, discontinued in 1909, were restored in 1918 to the cutoff of Mr. Lincolns sleeve. A genuine 1914-D will not show these letters (VDB) under the cutoff. On an altered coin they will most likely have been removed. In that event the truncation will definitely show burnish, file, or solder marks.

Caution: If the coin is sharp and your examinations prove out each of the checking processes, request an authentication slip from the seller. If this is not available, have the coin authenticated by one of the more reputable firms devoted to that profession.

103

The 1922-Broken D

The 1922 Lincoln Head cent without the mint letter D is the highest-value coin in the Lincoln series and the first accidental rarity in the minor coinage.

The only cent struck in 1922, it was minted at the Denver mint, but a filled die produced an unknown amount without the mint mark D. Some have part of the letter showing, which accounts for the reference "broken D," but in time the die filled completely, leaving the area under the date blank.

1922 Altered Date

Any such rarity or scarcity caused by the absence of a numeral or letter creates a whole new world for the "faker," or should. Actually, a coin with a symbol or character missing is more difficult to duplicate than one with all its components accounted for.

Warning: A 1922 cent with the D removed is readily detectable by the most inexperienced observer.

It is absolutely impossible to relieve a mint letter without damaging the surface of the coin. If the process can be accomplished with no evidence of a file, scraper, emery, grinder, or acid, it will leave a depression in its stead that can be detected with the naked eye or by the aid of a reading glass.

Note: The value of this particular coin makes it almost mandatory that even the perfect specimen be authenticated.

ONE CENT SMALL (LINCOLN HEAD), 1943

Specifics

U.S. Coin No: 18
Type: VI Small Cent
Size: 12 or ¾″
Weight: 42.5 grains
Edge: Plain

Composition: Zinc-coated steel
Quantity minted: 1,093,838,670
Proofs minted: None
Mint marks: D and s
Designer: Victor D. Brenner

Description

Obverse: The face of the wartime steel cent is the same as that of previous Lincoln one-cent pieces. The features are sharp only because the extra force needed to strike a steel planchet was added to the amount of pressure normally used to strike a bronze cent.

Bronze 1943 cents have been authenticated although fake specimens are known to exist in abundant quantities. Care should be exercised in acquiring any bronze copy as this is one piece counterfeiters found easy to duplicate. They have been die-struck, altered, and cast.

A magnet will soon determine whether or not the coin in question is a genuine bronze cent or a copperplated steel cent. If the composition proves to be other than steel, check the last two numerals. They could be "laid on" from other coins and the figure "3" "chased" from a figure "2" or "4."

ONE CENT SMALL (LINCOLN HEAD), 1944-1945

Specifics

U.S. Coin No: 19
Type: VII Small Cent
Size: 12 or ¾″
Weight: 48 grains
Edge: Plain

Composition: 95% copper, 5% zinc
Quantity minted: 3,597,291,000
Proofs Minted: None
Mint marks: D and S
Designer: Victor D. Brenner

Description

Both the Type VI and Type VII Lincoln Head cents were wartime emergency coins. Copper was the critical material during that period, and when the steel cent failed as a practical circulating medium in 1943, the 1944 cent was authorized to be struck from "shell casing" metal. This bronze alloy lacked only the two and one-half percent tin normally part of the regular Lincoln Cent composition.

Its only known contribution to the unauthorized chapter in U.S. coinage is its adaptability to the altering of 1914-D one-cent pieces.

Perhaps it should be noted here that the consideration given to the alloying of emergency or subsidiary coinage is based largely on the performance of that composition in vending machines. No other application has had quite the effect on the selection of proper portions of various base metals for coinage as has this single industry.

This alloy was made the legal composition for the Lincoln Cent in 1962.

The Double-Struck 1955 Cent

The 1955 Double-Struck Lincoln Cent is rightfully the second accidental rarity and the third-highest-value coin in the entire one-cent series.

While many of the known die errors involve only the date or mint mark, the Double-Struck 1955 Cent has two complete and distinct impressions of the obverse design, with one sufficiently rotated from the other to provide two of each letter and numeral, as well as doubled features in the profile.

Caution: Like the preceding scarce and rare dates, the 1955 double-die variety has managed to join the select group of known "fakes." Many of the pieces being sold today have been identified as die-struck counterfeits made in Milan, Italy. The increasing demand for this coin will undoubtedly create similar sources of supply in the near future.

However acquired, specimens of this particular date should be authenticated before a change in ownership or placing in a collector's cabinet. The penalty for possessing an unauthorized copy of any United States coin can be equivalent to the penalty for making such a coin, and could amount to a fine of five thousand dollars and fifteen years in prison.

There is no area of reasoning that justifies a "bargain" or "clearance" sale selling price for a coin of this scarcity. Under no circumstances, offer, buy, offer to buy, or consider buying any high-value coin that is not accompanied by documentary proof of its genuineness.

The proper procedures for having a coin verified are outlined fully in the section of this book entitled "Counterfeit and Unauthorized Coins."

ONE CENT SMALL (MEMORIAL LINCOLN), 1959-to date

Specifics

U.S. Coin No: 20
Type: **VIII** Small Cent
Size: 12 or ¾"
Weight: 48 grains
Edge: Plain

Composition: 95% copper, 5% tin/zinc
  1962 to date: 95% copper, 5% zinc
Quantity minted: 24,655,800,237
Proofs minted: 16,113,563
Mint marks: D and S
Designers: Victor D. Brenner
          Frank Gasparro

Description

The new one-cent Memorial reverse was designed by Frank Gasparro and approved by President Eisenhower on January 2, 1959, in observance of the 150th anniversary of Lincoln's birth.

The memorial occupies the center with the issuing authority in radius above and the denomination ONE CENT in radius below. The motto E PLURIBUS UNUM is centered above the device.

This is the first U.S. coin to ever carry the likeness of the same person on both sides, and to include the initials of two designers. Gasparro's initials FG are located to the right of the base.

FG

The Small-Date 1960 Lincoln Cent

Just recently the mint assumed the practice of cutting the date onto the model and transferring it to the hub along with the profile. Prior policy was to hand stamp the working die.

When a design does not change from one year to the next, the mint uses the old hub, erasing part of the date. For example, to create a die for 1959, the last digit is removed from the 1958 hub, a master is struck and the figure "9" stamped in place.

A hub is raised from the new master die, hardened, and used to produce any number of working dies on the multiplying press. Since the 1960 date required two new digits, the entire date was removed and four new numerals were applied to the master die.

It was in this phase of the operation that the small- and large-size numeral punches were used. This created a demand for the smaller of the two dates, since there were fewer of these pieces minted.

Illustrated Comparison

Small Date   **Large Date**

The figures "1," "9," and "6" should compare with the same numerals in a 1956 cent. The "0" is very close to the "0" in 1950.

The figure "1" as a bearing point shows the remaining numerals to be higher and lower at the letter line.

TWO-CENT PIECE, 1864-1873

Specifics

U.S. Coin No: 21
Type: I
Sizes: 14 or ⅞"
Weight: 96 grains
Edge: Plain

Composition: 95% copper, 5% tin/zinc
Quantity minted: 45,601,000
Proofs minted: 1,100 (1873 record)
Mint marks: None
Designer: James Longacre

Description

Obverse: Like most of his designs for minor coinage during this period, designer James Longacre created an ornate United States shield for the Two-Cent Piece. It was superimposed over a pair of crossed arrows and flanked on either side by thickly leafed branches of laurel. The motto IN GOD WE TRUST appeared, for the first time on any United States coin, in a scrolled ribbon above the shield assembly. The date was in radius in the base.

Reverse: Two agricultural half-wreaths of wheat, tied at the bottom by a bowless knot, involve the large figure "2" over CENTS. The inscription UNITED STATES OF AMERICA is circumscribed between the device and the embattled border pattern.

Authorized by the Act of April 22, 1864, the Two-Cent Piece was discontinued by the Act of February 12, 1873.

The Two-Cent Piece

The public accepted the new composition Two-Cent coin along with the new bronze One-Cent Piece in 1864. The hoarding of the "white" penny or Nickel Cent caused considerable shortage in commercial transactions and anything would be a relief to the silver Three-Cent Piece dilemma.

Longacre's design for the new Five-Cent Piece of 1866 bears a shield device closely resembling that of the Two-Cent Piece, and was accepted on the assumption that the shield was recognized as a symbol ". . . emblematic of Liberty."

The Congressional act providing for the new bronze coins determined their legal status for the first time. The cent would be accepted up to ten cents and the new Two-Cent Piece up to twenty cents.

Two different varieties were minted in 1864, which could affect the value of a coin of that date.

The first and highest-value variety displayed small letters in the motto and the second variety contained larger letters. On circulated pieces this difference can still be defined by the open D in GOD on a scarce coin. The second and least valuable shows a closed D.

The Open D   **The Closed D**

THREE CENTS (LIBERTY HEAD), 1865-1889

Specifics

U.S. Coin No: 22
Type: I Three Cent (nickel)
Size: 11 or 11⁄16″
Weight: 30 grains
Edge: Plain

Composition: 75% copper, 25% nickel
Quantity minted: 32,378,316
Proofs minted: 46,889
Mint marks: None
Designer: James Longacre

Description

Obverse: The profile of Liberty, facing left, with slightly longer tresses than the Indian Head profile, is nevertheless from the same model—his daughter, Sarah—used by Longacre on many of his works. The fall of hair sweeps back and down to a scroll below the neck truncation. It is held to the back of the head by a ribbon from the beaded coronet, inscribed with the word LIBERTY.

The issuing authority UNITED STATES OF AMERICA circumvents the device from the forward tip of the neck pedestal to the curled ends of the hair, and the date is in radius below the device.

Reverse: The denomination is symbolically indicated with a large Roman III inside a wreath of laurel. The borders are embattled denticles and there are no other markings on the field.

THREE CENTS (SINGLE-LINE STAR), 1851-1853

Specifics

U.S. Coin No: 23
Type: I Three Cent (silver)
Size: 9 or 9/16"
Weight: 12⅜ grains
Edge: Plain

Composition: 75% silver, 25% copper
Quantity minted: 36,230,090
Proofs minted: None
Mint marks: O-1851 only
Designer: James Longacre

Description

Obverse: The six-point star is distinguished from Types II and III by a single configuration line. It is imposed by a stylized United States shield. Ridge lines radiate visibly to each point. The device is circumscribed by UNITED STATES OF AMERICA and the date in the base.

Reverse: The denomination is indicated by the Roman numeral III involved in an ornate letter c, which is separated from the plain border by thirteen six-point stars.

THREE CENTS (TRIPLE-LINE STAR), 1854-1858

Specifics

U.S. Coin No: 24
Type: II Three Cent (silver)
Size: 9 or 9/16″
Weight: 11.52 grains
Edge: Plain

Composition: 90% silver, 10% copper
Quantity minted: 4,914,000
Proofs minted: None of record
Mint marks: None
Designer: James Longacre

Description

Obverse: The Type II Three-Cent Piece is essentially the same as Type I except for the triple configuration line of the star. On Types I and II the top point of the star is directly in line with the letter E in STATES.

Reverse: The original design remained untouched but a small sprig of laurel was inserted above the Roman numeral III and a bundle of three arrows added below. This was to show a reduction both in weight and intrinsic value and thus discourage exportation.

The legal tender limit of the silver Three-Cent Piece was a maximum of thirty cents, making it the only silver coin without unlimited quantity value.

James Longacre was select in his choice of symbols, making sure they conformed to law. He objected, however, to having to work in such low relief and proposed a thicker coin.

114

THREE CENTS (DOUBLE-LINE STAR), 1859-1873

Specifics

U.S. Coin No: 25
Type: III Three Cent (silver)
Size: 9 or 9/16″
Weight: 11.52 grains
Edge: Plain

Composition: 90% silver, 10% copper
Quantity minted: 1,581,490
Proofs minted: 10,040
Mint marks: None
Designer: James Longacre

Description

Obverse: Apparently the third issue of the small silver coin required a new obverse die. The motif and the device remained unaltered but the star had only two configuration lines. The inscription UNITED STATES OF AMERICA was in a smaller type face and was repositioned. The top point of the star is aimed at the last letter s in STATES; the lower left point lies between the U and N in UNITED and the right lower point pierces the space between the C and the A in AMERICA.

The reverse was unchanged.

In 1851, when Congress reduced the postage rate from five to three cents, small change lighter than the large copper Half Cents and One-Cent Pieces was necessary to facilitate the sale of postage. The Three-Cent Piece was authorized by the Act of March 3, 1851, and discontinued by that of February 12, 1873.

FIVE CENTS (SHIELD), 1866-1867

Specifics

U.S. Coin No: 26
Type: I Five Cent (nickel)
Size: 13 or 13⁄16″
Weight: 77.16 grains
Edge: Plain

Composition: 75% copper, 25% nickel
Quantity minted: 14,950,000 (approx.)
Proofs minted: Record incomplete
Mint marks: None
Designer: James Longacre

Description

Obverse: Since this coin was designed by Longacre a year after he prepared the Two-Cent Piece, it is natural that the two devices are similar. The highly ornamental Union shield dominates the center. Two arrows are crossed at the base and two laurel branches turn downward from either side. It is topped with the pattée cross. The motto IN GOD WE TRUST accompanies the denticled border at the top and the date is in radius in the base.

Reverse: Thirteen stars and thirteen rays are arranged intermittently around a large numeral "5." Curved around the stylized glory is the inscription UNITED STATES OF AMERICA and the word CENTS is separated from the inscription by a dot on each side.

All in all, it was a design not well accepted by the public, and shortly after the 1867 issue was under way, Longacre removed the rays.

116

FIVE CENTS (SHIELD), 1867-1883

Specifics

U.S. Coin No: 27
Type: II Five Cent (nickel)
Size: 13 or 1³⁄₁₆″
Weight: 77.16 grains
Edge: Plain

Composition: 75% copper, 25% nickel
Quantity minted: 111,413,949
Proofs minted: 23,099
Mint marks: None
Designer: James Longacre

Description

Obverse: The height of the type face was reduced in the motto. Other than that, the balance of the design remained the same as that of Type I.

Reverse: Except that it had no rays, this motif also remained unaltered.

The Five-Cent minor coin was authorized by the Act of May 16, 1866, to contain the copper-nickel alloy, and was to weigh 77.16 grains. This has never changed except during the emergency period in World War II. There were no further alterations until the design was discarded for the Liberty Head of 1883.

Note: The cross surmounting the shield is a pattée, described in the rules of heraldry as having the outer edges flat. The Maltese cross with which it is erroneously identified has dovetailed outer surfaces and eight points symbolizing the eight beatitudes.

117

FIVE CENTS (LIBERTY HEAD), 1883

Specifics

U.S. Coin No: 28
Type: III Five Cent (nickel)
Size: 13 or 13⁄16″
Weight: 77.16 grains
Edge: Plain

Composition: 75% copper, 25% nickel
Quantity minted: 5,479,519
Proofs minted: 5,219
Mint marks: None
Designer: Charles E. Barber

The absence of the word CENTS on the reverse of this nickel caused it to become the most famous of misdesigned and misused coins.

Racketeer Nickels[1] got their name from being gold-plated and passed as Half Eagles. Nothing on the piece gave a hint as to its denomination.

Some coins have reeded edges. These are products of facilities outside the mint.

[1] This is an illegal coin.

118

FIVE CENTS (LIBERTY HEAD), 1883-1912 (1913)

Specifics

U.S. Coin No: 29
Type: IV Five Cent (nickel)
Size: 13 or 13/16″
Weight: 77.16 grains
Edge: Plain

Composition: 75% copper, 25% nickel
Quantity minted: 99,197,920
Proofs minted: 79,921
Mint marks: s and d (1912 only)
Designer: Charles E. Barber

Description

Obverse: Liberty faces left, her hair secured at the back by a self-contained knot. Behind the coronet, inscribed with LIBERTY, is a spray of cotton and wheat. Thirteen stars encircle the device, with the date in the base.

Reverse: Two half-wreaths of corn, cotton, wheat, and tobacco involve a Roman numeral v, with UNITED STATES OF AMERICA in radius above and the word CENTS in radius below. The motto E PLURIBUS UNUM is relocated between the wreath and the inscription.

The 1913 is not an official issue, but five were struck and are accounted for.

119

FIVE CENTS (INDIAN HEAD), Buffalo, 1913

Specifics

U.S. Coin No: 30
Type: V Five Cent (nickel)
Size: 13 or 13⁄16″
Weight: 77.16 grains
Edge: Plain

Composition: 75% copper, 25% nickel
Quantity minted: 38,435,520
Proofs minted: 3,034
Mint marks: D and S
Designer: James E. Fraser

Description

Obverse: Fraser designed the composite American Indian profile from models Chief John Big Tree, a Seneca; Chief Two Moons, a Cheyenne; and Chief Iron Tail, a Sioux. This coin is the only one in the entire series completely devoid of heraldic symbols and is referred to as the "typically American design." LIBERTY is in radius between two and three o'clock; the date is on the shoulder; and Fraser's initial F is below the date.

FIVE CENTS (INDIAN HEAD), Buffalo, 1913-1938

Specifics

U.S. Coin No: 31
Type: VI Five Cent (nickel)
Size: 13 or 13⁄16″
Weight: 77.16 grains
Edge: Plain

Composition: 75% copper, 25% nickel
Quantity minted: 1,174,084,709
Proofs minted: 13,114
Mint marks: D and s
Designer: James E. Fraser

Description

Reverse: On the Type V Five-Cent Piece, the mound under the Buffalo was too high, causing the denomination to wear quickly and interfere with the stacking. This was corrected on Type VI by putting the words FIVE CENTS and the mint mark in exergue, thus reducing the mound to a plane.

The Bison (Buffalo) device occupies the larger portion of the field with his forelock, tail, and right hind fetlock touching the plain inside border.

The denomination FIVE CENTS on the mound of Type V is slightly off center to the right, while the same denomination is larger and centered under the plane on Type VI, and touches the inside border at both ends of the lower letter line.

The issuing authority, UNITED STATES OF AMERICA, is inscribed in the upper border radius, with the motto E PLURIBUS UNUM forced between the word AMERICA and the buffalo's back.

The Three-Legged Buffalo

A desirable high-value piece in the Indian Head series is the Three-Legged Buffalo. It shows no right front leg between the knee and the hoof. This occurred when the die was being dressed down after being damaged during the coining process.

Other outlines and configuration changes cancel out the theory that a broken or filled die was responsible for this phenomenon.

Not all three-legged specimens are genuine, however. The leg has been removed on several "hot" sale items and should be examined for any signs of hand tooling.

Two-Feathered Indian

A second example of a missing component is the "two-feathered" variety in which the third or last feather tip has completely disappeared from the base of the head. It is easy to see how the die cavity would fill at the apex where the hair and feather meet. This, too, bears watching since it could be an alteration.

The 1918 over 1917

This is the highest-value coin in this series. The outline of the numeral "7" is plainly visible behind the overdate "8." The complexities of this overstrike make it improbable to duplicate, but pieces offered at extremely low prices or under secret circumstances should be validated.

FIVE CENTS (JEFFERSON HEAD), 1938-1942, 1946-to date

Specifics

U.S. Coin No: 32
Type: VII Jefferson (Nickel)
Size: 13 or 1³⁄₁₆″
Weight: 77.16 grains
Edge: Plain

Composition: 75% copper, 25% nickel
Quantity minted: 7,937,666,656
Proofs minted: 19,931,995
Mint marks: D and S
Designer: Felix Schlag

Description

Obverse: Thomas Jefferson's profile faces left, with the motto IN GOD WE TRUST in radius inside the left rim, and LIBERTY followed by the date inside the right rim. They are separated by a five-point star.

Reverse: Jefferson's home, Monticello, maintains the area from left to

right with MONTICELLO inscribed under the base. The denomination FIVE CENTS and the issuing authority, UNITED STATES OF AMERICA, are in radius in the lower rim with the motto E PLURIBUS UNUM in radius at the top.

Mint marks D or S are positioned above the right base end on all coins minted from 1938 to 1942 and 1946 to 1964.

FIVE CENTS (JEFFERSON HEAD), 1942-1945

Specifics

U.S. Coin No: 33
Type: VIII Jefferson Nickel
Size: 13 or 13⁄16″
Weight: 77.16
Edge: Plain

Composition: WWII emergency— 56% copper, 35% silver, 9% manganese
Quantity minted: 869,923,700
Proofs minted: 27,000 (1942 only)
Mint marks: P, D, and S
Designer: Felix Schlag

Description

Obverse: Identical to the previous type. Felix Schlag's winning suggestion won him $1,000 in competition with 390 other artists. Mr. Schlag's model was a photograph found in an old magazine in one of Chicago's secondhand bookstores.

Reverse: The front elevation of Monticello was suggested by President Franklin D. Roosevelt as the ideal motif for the new coin. It was unchanged during the emergency period except for relocation of the mint letters.

The need for nickel and copper during World War II made it necessary to alter the composition in our minor coinage. Five-Cent Pieces were being minted at the Philadelphia and Denver facilities when the emergency bill was passed. For the first time in our coinage history, the letter P designating Philadelphia was affixed to a coin.

The Wartime Five-Cent Piece

All silver Five-Cent Pieces bear a large mint letter—P, D, or s—immediately above the dome of Monticello. The dies were distributed when the directive came through to change the reverse, but Denver was still tooled for the 1942 regular issue and did not mint silver coins until the beginning of 1943.

D Mint   S Mint

The Flagpole or Dollar Sign

The first public concern over the new "silver" coins came when a die break in the San Francisco reverse made the dome appear as though a flagpole had been added. Others found that the break changed the mint letter s to $, the dollar sign, which also created public interest. These pieces do command slightly higher consideration by special collectors.

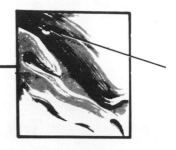

Check all 1939-D and 1950-D nickels for these defects, peculiar only to the unauthorized coin.

A few of both dates show this "pit" in Jefferson's hair.

Specimens of both the 1939-D and the 1950-D show a small dot between the A and the M in AMERICA.

The Counterfeit 1939-D and 1950-D Nickels (Cont'd.)

All fake 1950-D's have this small worm-type "blip" just off the leg of the R in the word TRUST. It is visible to the naked eye, but the use of a magnifying glass will establish verification.

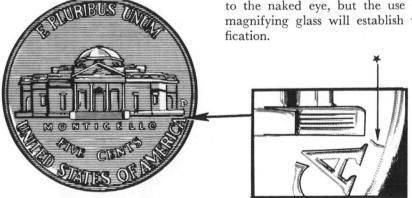

Some 1950-D's have a worm-shaped defect just inside the rim between the last A in AMERICA and the base of Monticello.

These coins are highly deceptive even under close examination. Their weight and dimensions fall within mint tolerances. They are, however, struck on planchets of 70% copper and 30% nickel alloy as contrasted to the 75-25 ratio of a genuine coin.

Most of the counterfeit 1939-D and 1950-D nickels examined have a "gunmetal gray" coloration. A questionable nickel should be verified if there are indications one or more of these defects have been removed.

Every coin issued after the turn of the century bore the initials of the designer with the exception of the Jefferson Five-Cent Piece. Mr. Schlag, being a modest man, never presumed the honor he felt should be extended by the government. In 1966, when *Coin World* urged the addition of the designer's initials, they were added just below the sleeve cutoff.

Due to a hurriedly enacted coinage-control policy, all reference to the minting facility was omitted from United States coinage from 1965 to 1968. In 1968 the mint letter D was located on the obverse between the hair scroll and last digit in the date. Proof sets issued that year had the letter s for the San Francisco facility of the United States Assay Office in the same area.

107 West Exchange Street
Owosso, Michigan 48867
December 31, 1965

Mr. Mort Reed
Odd and Curious
Box 555
Wooster, Ohio

Dear Mr. Reed:

   I read your Odd and Curious every week with the greatest of interest.

   On the enclosed Dec. 29 issue, I marked two places for the possibility of placing my initials on the Jefferson Nickel. The lower right corner would be preferable.

   As far as I can recall, I have my initials $\frac{F}{S}$ only on a few pieces of my work.

   But my part in the movement to place my initials on the coin is absolutely neutral. Nevertheless it is extremely heartwarming that it was suggested.

   Thanking you for your interest, I am

                              Sincerely yours

                              Felix Schlag

                              Felix Schlag

HALF DIME (FLOWING HAIR), 1794-1795

Specifics

U.S. Coin No: 34
Type: I Half Dime
Size: 10 or 5⁄8″
Weight: 20.8 grains
Edge: Reeded

Composition: 892.4 fine silver
Quantity minted: 86,416
Proofs minted: None of record
Mint marks: None
Designer: Probably Robert Scot

Description

The Act of April 2, 1792, authorized the issuance of the Half Dime, but it was not minted until 1794. The mintage total shown in the specifics is for the years 1794 and 1795.

Obverse: The main device is LIBERTY facing right. Neither coronet nor headband identifies her. The shoulder-length fall of hair is directed down and toward the back. The inscription LIBERTY is in radius above; the date in radius below. Eight stars accompany the left inside border, and seven, the right inside border.

Reverse: A "small" eagle completely enveloped in two half-wreaths of laurel ties with a bowless knot. The inscription UNITED STATES OF AMERICA fills the area between the wreath and the border denticles.

Note: File marks on the edges of early silver coinage are natural-adjustment serrations made during the final weighing.

HALF DIME (DRAPED BUST/SMALL EAGLE), 1796-1797

Specifics

U.S. Coin No: 35
Type: II Half Dime
Size: 10 or ⅝"
Weight: 20.8 grains
Edge: Reeded

Composition: 892.4 silver, 107.6 copper
Quantity minted: 54,757
Proofs minted: None of record
Mint marks: None
Designer: Gilbert Stuart

Description

Obverse: During this period Liberty took on a more recognizable image and started looking less symbolic. Her tresses fall beyond shoulder length and end in a scroll in front of the date. Temple strands are drawn back and secured by a ribbon and double bow, while shorter pieces are arranged on the forefront. A drape in folds covers the bust and shoulders. LIBERTY is inscribed in the legend and the date in the base. Both are separated left and right by six-point stars totaling thirteen, sixteen, or fifteen in number, with no particular quantity for a given date.

Reverse: An awkward likeness of an eagle fledgling with raised wings stands on a mound within a wreath of half laurel and palm. The surrounding inscription UNITED STATES OF AMERICA closely duplicates the previous issue. There is no indication of denomination on this type designed by Stuart.

The border pattern on both sides is made up of extended denticles.

131

HALF DIME (DRAPED BUST/HERALDIC EAGLE), 1800-1805

Specifics

U.S. Coin No: 36
Type: III Half Dime
Size: 10 or ⅝"
Weight: 20.8 grains
Edge: Reeded

Composition: 892.4 silver,
107.6 copper
Quantity minted: 124,370
Proofs minted: none of record
Mint marks: none
Designers: Robert Scot
Gilbert Stuart

Description

Obverse: This series retained the previous bust of Liberty, with the same position of LIBERTY and date, separated by seven stars on the left and six stars on the right. The denomination does not appear on this type.

Reverse: The influence of the Great Seal of the United States can be seen in the device on this type. The American bald eagle is displayed holding a bundle of thirteen arrows in his right talon and an olive sprig in his left, the Union shield on his breast, and in his beak, a scroll bearing the motto E PLURIBUS UNUM. An arc of six cloud puffs from the right to the left wing enclose a constellation of thirteen six-point stars. Circumscribed within the radius of the border is the issuing authority, UNITED STATES OF AMERICA, interrupted at ten and two o'clock by the wing tips. The border pattern is of extended denticles.

HALF DIME (LIBERTY CAP), 1829-1837

Specifics

U.S. Coin No: 37
Type: IV Half Dime
Size: 10 or ⅝"
Weight: 20.8 grains
Edge: Reeded

Composition: 892.4 silver,
107.6 copper
Quantity minted: 14,463,700
Proofs minted: None of record
Mint marks: None
Designer: John Reich

Description

Obverse: A distinct departure from preceding designs. Liberty faces left wearing a Phrygian slave's cap inscribed with the word LIBERTY. Small tufts of hair protrude from under the edge of the cap with excessive shoulder-length tresses scrolled between the shoulder cutoff and the last two digits in the date. Seven six-point stars curve within the left border from the breast to the top of the forehead, and six curve from the hair scroll to the back of the head.

Reverse: A disproportionate eagle with inverted wings figures in the device, holding in his talons an olive sprig to his right and three broad-head arrows to his left. In radius immediately above is a scroll bearing the motto E PLURIBUS UNUM, and the device is circumscribed from wing tip to the arrows with UNITED STATES OF AMERICA. Denomination is indicated for the first time in the Half-Dime series with a numeral "5" and the letter c. The border is a beaded pattern.

133

HALF DIME (LIBERTY SEATED), 1837-1838

Specifics

U.S. Coin No: 38
Type: V Half Dime
*Size*s 10 or ⅝″
Weight: 20.625 grains
Edge: Reeded

Composition: 90% silver,
10% copper
Quantity minted: 2,255,000
Proofs minted: None of record
Mint marks: o (1838 only)
Designer: Christian Gobrecht

Description

The weight and fineness of the Half Dime were changed by the Act of January 18, 1837.

Obverse: Gobrecht's figure of Liberty seated faces the left. Her fall of shoulder-length hair is neatly confined by a small fillet at the base of the head. The loose gown, held by shoulder straps, clings to the legs and then falls free at the base of the rock on which she braces the Union shield. A scroll, bearing the word LIBERTY, extends under the sinister base of the shield. In her right hand, she holds a staff topped by the slave's cap. No further inscriptions or markings appear on the surface.

Reverse: In conformity with the Act of January 18, 1837, the eagle was replaced by the two half-wreaths of laurel involving the denomination HALF DIME, tied by a ribbon and double bow. The issuing authority, UNITED STATES OF AMERICA, separates the device from the beaded border pattern.

HALF DIME (LIBERTY SEATED), 1838-1860

Specifics

U.S. Coin No: 39
Type: VI Half Dime
Size: 10 or ⅝″
Weight: 20.625 grains 1838
      19.2 grains 1853-1860
Edge: Reeded

Composition: 90% silver,
      10% copper
Quantity minted: 20,700,000
      22,860,020 with
      arrows
Proofs minted: None of record
Mint marks: o only
Designer: Christian Gobrecht

Description

Obverse: The weight of the Half Dime was changed by the Act of February 21, 1853, and from late 1853 to 1855, arrows flanked the date. The seated figure of Liberty is on a smaller rock, and the shield has been straightened to a complete vertical position. The scroll, inscribed with LIBERTY, and the pole and cap are essentially the same as Type V.

An arc of seven six-point stars occupy the field to the left, and six arc the field to the right with one separated from the pattern by the slave's cap.

Reverse: The motif is identical to the previous type, with the mint letter o placed between the M in DIME and the double bow on those coins minted in New Orleans. The border pattern consists of embattled denticles.

The arrows were removed from the obverse in 1856.

HALF DIME (LIBERTY SEATED), 1859-1860

Specifics

U.S. Coin No: None
Type: Transitional Half Dime
Size: 10 or ⅝″
Weight: 19.2 grains
Edge: Reeded

Composition: 90% silver,
    10% copper
Quantity minted: 100
Proofs minted: None of record
Mint marks: None
Designer: Christian Gobrecht

Description

Obverse: A transition piece is a pattern of a proposed issue containing either the obverse or reverse design of an existing issue, backed by a new design for the opposite side.

In this coin, the obverse is retained while a new design has been added to its reverse. The type face for the denomination HALF DIME has been reduced and is surrounded by two half-wreaths of the nation's four leading agricultural products—corn, cotton, tobacco, and wheat—tied at their stems by a ribbon and double bow.

The wreath occupies the entire area to the border pattern of embattled denticles. There is no reference to the issuing authority.

Essentially this piece is a test pattern and ordinarily does not go into circulation. The transitional coin or pattern is a complete study in itself.

HALF DIME (LIBERTY SEATED), 1860-1873

Specifics

U.S. Coin No: 40
Type: VII Half Dime
Size: 10 or ⅝"
Weight: 19.2 grains
Edge: Milled

Composition: 90% silver,
    10% copper
Quantity minted: 15,563,240
Proofs minted: 10,040
Mint marks: s and o
Designer: Christian Gobrecht

Description

Obverse: This coin is identical to the transitional piece, except for the issuing authority, UNITED STATES OF AMERICA, which is divided and flanks the main device on the left and right.

Reverse: Identical to the transitional piece, with mint marks located normally between the M in DIME and the double bow. One variety of the 1872 San Francisco issue has the mint letter s below the wreath.

The Half Dime was discontinued by the Act of February 12, 1873.

ONE DIME (DRAPED BUST / SMALL EAGLE), 1796-1797

Specifics

U.S. Coin No: 41
Type: I Dime
Size: 13 or 13⁄16″
Weight: 41.6 grains
Edge: Reeded

Composition: 892.4 silver,
107.6 copper
Quantity minted: 47,396
Proofs minted: None of record
Mint marks: None
Designer: Gilbert Stuart

Description

Obverse: The Dime was authorized by the Coinage Act of April 2, 1792, but was not coined until 1796.

The obverse design is similar to the Half Dime of the same year. The draped bust of Liberty, facing right, is flanked by two opposing curved rows of six-point stars—eight to the left and seven to the right.

The legend LIBERTY is in radius at the top but confined to a smaller area than the same legend on the Half Dime. Varieties of the 1797 issue show sixteen and thirteen stars, which have no particular significance to the meaning of the design.

Reverse: The motif is the same as the Half Dime except for a larger mound supporting the eagle. The lower inside palm leaves are longer on the Half Dime where they turn in under the wing. The denomination is not indicated on this piece.

ONE DIME (DRAPED BUST/HERALDIC EAGLE), 1798-1807

Specifics

U.S. Coin No: 42

Type: II Dime

Size: 13 or 13/16″

Weight: 41.6 grains

Edge: Reeded

Composition: 892.4 silver,
107.6 copper

Quantity minted: 422,010

Proofs minted: None of record

Mint marks: None

Designer: Robert Scot

Description

Obverse: The profile of Liberty faces right and is essentially the same as U.S. Coin No. 41. It is flanked by a curved pattern of seven stars on the left and six on the right, with the date in the base.

Reverse: The small eagle disclosed is replaced by the heraldic eagle of the United States seal, bearing the Union shield on its breast and holding a bundle of thirteen arrows in the right talon and an olive branch in the left. This latter arrangement has serious heraldic implications in that the war arrow in a dexter talon shows a preference for conflict. This was corrected on future devices of the same symbols.

One variety of this 1798 coin contains thirteen stars above the eagle and a second variety has sixteen. A variety of 1804 contains fourteen stars under the six cloud puffs. The motto E PLURIBUS UNUM is inscribed on the scroll held in the eagle's beak, and the issuing authority, UNITED STATES OF AMERICA, involves the design from the arrows to the olive sprig.

ONE DIME (LIBERTY CAP), 1809-1837

Specifics

U.S. Coin No: 43
Type: III Dime
Size: 12 or ¾"
Weight: 41.6 grains
Edge: Reeded

Composition: 892.4 silver,
107.6 copper
Quantity minted: 12,386,329
Proofs minted: None of record
Mint marks: None
Designers: John Reich,
Robert Scot

Description

Obverse: The design is closely identified with that on U.S. Coin No. 37. Liberty, wearing the ancient symbol of freed slaves—the Phrygian cap— faces left. Her shoulder-length tresses are considerably fuller than those in profile on the Half Dime. On some specimens these scrolled hair tufts almost touch the last of the six stars on the right; on others, they appear to close the gap between the star and the last digit in the date. The correct count of thirteen stars is balanced out with a curved row on the left of the device.

Reverse: Once again, the disproportionate eagle serves as the main symbol, with a head noticeably larger in proportion to the rest of his body. A Union shield covers his breast and an arched scroll bearing the motto E PLURIBUS UNUM is subordinate to the inscription UNITED STATES OF AMERICA in the legend. An olive branch and three broad-head arrows lie horizontally in the grasp of the eagle's talons. The denomination 10c is immediately below the eagle.

ONE DIME (LIBERTY SEATED), 1837-1838

Specifics

U.S. Coin No: 44
Type: IV Dime
Size: 11 or $^{11}/_{16}''$
Weight: 41.25 grains
Edge: Reeded

Composition: 90% silver,
10% copper
Quantity minted: 402,434
Proofs minted: None of record
Mint marks: o
Designer: Christian Gobrecht

Description

Obverse: The plain field of the obverse is disturbed only by the figure of Liberty seated on a large rock, holding a staff topped with a Phrygian slave's cap in her left hand and supporting a Union shield with her right. A scroll, leading from her right hand and inscribed with the word LIBERTY, crosses downward to the sinister base of the shield. No other marks appear on the obverse except the date in exergue.

Reverse: Changes in the weight and fineness of the Dime were authorized by the Act of January 18, 1837, of which Section 13 specifically called for the omission of the eagle on the reverse of the Half Dime and Dime. Designed by Gobrecht, the Type IV Dime replaced the eagle with the large denomination ONE DIME surrounded by two half-wreaths of laurel and tied at the stem end with a ribbon and double bow.

As in previous types, the issuing authority, UNITED STATES OF AMERICA, all but encircles the device. The border pattern is beaded.

ONE DIME (LIBERTY SEATED), 1838-1860

Specifics

U.S. Coin No: 45
Type: V Dime
Size: 11 or $^{11}/_{16}''$
Weight: 41.25 grains 1838
      38.4 grains 1853-1860
Edges: Reeded

Composition: 90% silver,
      10% copper
Quantity minted: 72,820,744
Proofs minted: Rare
Mint marks: o and s
Designer: Christian Gobrecht

Description

Obverse: Following the type order of the Half Dime, the Dime type for this period retained the seated figure of Liberty as the main device but flanked her with curved patterns of six-point stars on the left and on the right. The seven stars are consistent and to Liberty's right, while the six stars are interrupted by the pole and cap on her left. The date between 1838 and 1841 is in radius in the base, and the shield is on an angle from center.

The Act of February 21, 1853, reduced the weight, and arrows were added on either side of the date until 1856.

On the 1840 coins the shield is positioned in a perfect vertical center, and the denomination ONE.DIME is displayed in two different type faces.

Two major varieties were created between 1838 and 1840; drapery at the apex of the left arm and leg appeared on some issues and not on others.

ONE DIME (THE CHRISTIAN GOBRECHT LIBERTY SEATED), 1859

Specifics

U.S. Coin No: None
Type: Transitional Dime
Size: 11 or 11⁄16″
Weight: 38.4 grains
Edge: Reeded

Composition: 90% silver,
10% copper
Quantity minted: Unavailable
Proofs minted: None
Mint marks: None
Designer: Christian Gobrecht

Description

Obverse: Like the Half Dime, the Dime went through a brief transitional period during which the obverse of the preceding year was matched with a new design for the reverse. This transitional piece retained the obverse of 1859 and adopted the reverse of 1860.

Reverse: The denomination ONE DIME is centered in two half-wreaths of agricultural products—corn, cotton, tobacco, and wheat—bound and tied near the stem with a ribbon and double bow. The device occupies the entire area to the beaded border.

No reference is made to the issuing authority, and there are no further marks on the field.

Transitional pieces are highly valued and rarely, if ever, found in circulation. Question the authenticity of such a coin if it is offered under other than valid conditions.

ONE DIME (LIBERTY SEATED), 1860-1891

Specifics

U.S. Coin No: 46
Type: VI Dime
Size: 11 or 11⁄16″
Weight: 38.4 grains 1860
    38.58 grains 1873-1891
Edge: Reeded

Composition: 90% silver,
    10% copper
Quantity minted: 181,959,408
Proofs minted: 46,803
Mint marks: O, S, and CC
Designer: Christian Gobrecht

Description

Obverse: Gobrecht's figure of Liberty seated faces left, with hair falling beyond shoulder length and neatly secured at the back of the head by a small fillet. A staff in her left hand is topped by a Phrygian slave's cap that all but touches the O in OF in the legend UNITED STATES OF AMERICA. Her right hand steadies the Union shield and grasps a scroll that crosses the shield diagonally to the sinister base, bearing the word LIBERTY. The date is straight in the base.

The Act of February 12, 1873, increased the weight of the Dime, and to indicate this increase, arrows were placed on either side of the date. They were removed in 1875.

Mint letters may be found inside and below the wreath of cotton, corn, tobacco, and wheat on pieces issued in 1875.

The border pattern is beaded.

ONE DIME (LIBERTY HEAD), Barber, 1892-1916

Specifics

U.S. Coin No: 47
Type: VII Dime
Size: 11 or ¹¹⁄₁₆″
Weight: 38.58 grains
Edge: Reeded

Composition: 90% silver,
10% copper
Quantity minted: 503,263,328
Proofs minted: 17,343
Mint marks: o, s, and D
Designer: Charles E. Barber

Description

Obverse: Liberty, facing right, wears the traditional slave's cap, crowned with a laurel wreath tied at the base of the head with a bowless knot. The issuing authority, UNITED STATES OF AMERICA, involves the head from the ribbon ends to a point just below the chin. The date is in the base.

Reverse: The denomination ONE DIME centers an agricultural wreath of corn, cotton, tobacco, and wheat. The mint letter is below the wreath.

Counterfeits of some high-value pieces are known to exist.

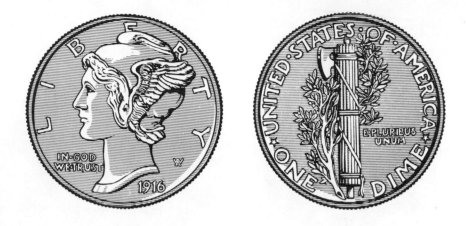

ONE DIME (WINGED LIBERTY HEAD "MERCURY")
1916-1945

Specifics

U.S. Coin No: 48
Type: VIII "Mercury" Dime
Size: 11 or 11⁄16″
Weight: 38.58 grains
Edge: Reeded

Composition: 90% silver,
    10% copper
Quantity minted: 2,677,941,528
Proofs minted: 78,648
Mint marks: D and S
Designer: A. A. Weinman

Description

Obverse: Liberty, facing left, wears a winged slave's cap symbolic of freedom of thought. Referred to as "Mercury Head." Tresses of hair form a scroll extending to the lead edge of the cap and tucked in at the ear lobes. The legend LIBERTY is letterspaced inside the plain border. The date is between the neck pedestal and the border. The motto IN GOD WE TRUST is inscribed below the chin.

Reverse: The fasces, a Roman symbol of authority, and the motto E PLURIBUS UNUM are completely circumvented by the issuing authority, UNITED STATES OF AMERICA and denomination.

The 1916-D Liberty Head Dime

There were only 264,000 pieces of this date struck at the Denver mint, which accounts for its rarity.

The mint letter D is located in the space to the left of the olive-branch stem and next to the E in ONE on the reverse.

Warning: Counterfeits have been made by "laying" the letter D, "lifted" from another coin, on this piece and "sweating" it firm. Examine the edge of the mint letter on a questionable piece. If it is black and ragged, it is undoubtedly a fake. Others have been made by "chasing" the metal of a similar date with a Denver mint letter.

Under no circumstance should a 1916-D Liberty Head Dime change ownership without proper authentication.

The 1942 over 1 Liberty Head Dime

The second high-value coin in this series is the 1942 over 1. The numeral "1" is clearly visible, "closing" the "2."

It was made by inadvertently using a hub dated 1941 during one of the striking operations in sinking a die.

Warning: These pieces are known to have been counterfeited by "laying on" a numeral over the "1," "chasing" a similar date, and just plain fabrication. All coins of overdate should be examined and verified before changing ownership.

Designer's Initials

The monogram between the Y in the Legend LIBERTY and the base of the neck is A under W, the mark of A. A. Weinman. His model was the wife of the celebrated poet Wallace Stevens.

ONE DIME (ROOSEVELT HEAD), 1946-1964

Specifics

U.S. Coin No: 49
Type: IX Dime
Size: 11 or $^{11}\!/_{16}$"
Weight: 38.58 grains
Edge: Reeded

Composition: 90% silver,
    10% copper
Quantity minted: 5,161,379,795
Proofs minted: 19,837,717
Mint Marks: D and S
Designer: John R. Sinnock

Description

Obverse: The main device is President Franklin Delano Roosevelt's profile. The legend LIBERTY appears on the plain border from immediately below the nose of the profile to a point opposite the hairline of the forehead.

The motto IN GOD WE TRUST is inscribed in a double line below the chin, and the date all but touches the truncation of the neck and the inner border at the base to the right of center.

Reverse: A vertical flaming torch is flanked on the left by a sprig of laurel, and on the right, by a sprig of oak. Inscribed from left to right is the motto E PLURIBUS UNUM, separated into E PLU/RIB/USU/NUM by the base of the torch and the two stems. The issuing authority, UNITED STATES OF AMERICA, and the denomination ONE DIME occupy the area within the plain border and are separated by a dot at each end of the motto.

The designer's initials, JS, may be found at the forward edge of the neck.

ONE DIME (ROOSEVELT HEAD) CLAD, 1965-to date

Specifics

U.S. Coin No: 50
Type: X Dime
Size: 11 or 11⁄16″
Weight: 35 grains
Edge: Reeded

Composition: See below
Quantity minted: 7,993,727,080*
Proofs minted: 8,608,950*
Mint marks: D (s-proofs only)
Designer: John R. Sinnock

Description

The Coinage Act of 1965 provided for the minting of a dime or ten-cent piece composed of an alloy of 75% copper and 25% nickel clad on a core of pure copper. The clad dime weighs 2.268 grams or 9.3% less than the silver piece of the same denomination.

Section 3 of the act provides specific recognition of the new coinage as legal tender of the United States. (See Appendix.)

Edge of Silver Dime

Edge of Clad Dime

*To 1970

TWENTY-CENT PIECE (LIBERTY SEATED), 1875-1878

Specifics

U.S. Coin No: 51
Type: I Twenty Cents
Size: 14 or ⅞″
Weight: 77.16 grains
Edge: Plain

Composition: 90% silver,
10% copper
Quantity minted: 1,355,000
Proofs minted: 3,460
Mint marks: s and cc
Designer: Christian Gobrecht

Description

Obverse: The conventional figure of Liberty seated holds in her left hand a staff topped by a Phrygian slave's cap. In her right hand, she supports a Union shield and holds a scroll that runs diagonally over the shield to the sinister and bears the word LIBERTY.

The date is in the base, and thirteen small six-point stars encircle the device from eight to four o'clock.

Reverse: An eagle displayed with inverted wings, holding in his right talon three broad-head arrows and in his left a sprig of olive.

The issuing authority, UNITED STATES OF AMERICA, and the denomination TWENTY CENTS, separated by two six-point stars, completely surround the device. The border is denticled. The mint letter is above the Y in the denomination.

Obverse of Twenty-Cent Piece   **Obverse of Quarter**

A Word About the Twenty-Cent Piece.

Its coinage was authorized by the Act of March 3, 1875, which also established a weight of 77.16 grains and a fineness of 90% fine silver. The coin, never popular because it was identified too closely with the quarter, was discontinued by the Act of May 2, 1878.

The high-value piece in the series is the 1876 CC as only ten thousand of these coins were minted. Most of the coins of this date were melted at the mint and so never entered circulation. A few did, however, and for that reason they are a desirable piece to the collector.

Warning: The value placed on the 1876 CC makes it profitable to duplicate it illegally.

Altered pieces are known to exist. The numeral "6" should be examined under a magnifying glass to determine if it has been "chased" from the numeral "5" on the 1875 CC. Authenticating firms are set up to do this.

Cast counterfeits are known to exist, too, and any Twenty-Cent coin of this date should be validated by the same expert laboratory processes before it changes ownership.

See Chapter XI, for methods of determining the visual and technical properties of a suspected fake.

QUARTER DOLLAR (DRAPED BUST), 1796

Specifics

U.S. Coin No: 52
Type: I Quarter Dollar
Size: 18 or 1⅛″
Weight: 104 grains
Edge: Reeded

Composition: 892.4 silver,
107.6 copper
Quantity minted: 6,146
Proofs minted: None of record
Mint marks: None
Designer: Robert Scot

Description

Obverse: Coinage of the Quarter Dollar was authorized by the Act of April 2, 1792, but it was not struck nor issued until four years later. Liberty faces right, her extreme fall of hair extending below the shoulder, with temple strands secured at the back of the head by a multi-bowed ribbon. The tufts on the top of the head are scrolled.

The word LIBERTY is inscribed in the legend, and the date is in the base. Eight six-point stars are in radius in the inside left border, and seven in the inside right border.

Reverse: A small disclosed eagle on a mound fills the area within the laurel sprig to the left of the coin and the palm branch on the right. Sprig and branch are bound into a wreath by a double-bowed ribbon.

The issuing authority, UNITED STATES OF AMERICA, completely encircles the device. The border patterns consist of extended denticles.

QUARTER DOLLAR (DRAPED BUST/HERALDIC EAGLE), 1804-1807

Specifics

U.S. Coin No: 53
Type: II Quarter Dollar
Size: 18 or 1⅛"
Weight: 104 grains
Edge: Reeded

Composition: 892.4 silver,
107.6 copper
Quantity minted: 554,899
Proofs minted: None of record
Mint marks: None
Designer: John Reich

Description

Obverse: The portrait of Liberty is intentionally identical to the previous type, except that it is less full in the face. The difference is sufficient for consideration when authenticating. When aligned with the legend LIBERTY, the date is off center to the left.

A radius pattern of seven six-point stars parallel the left border of the coin; a pattern of six, the right border.

Reverse: A heraldic eagle, influenced by the Great Seal, is displayed with a Union shield on his breast, a bundle of thirteen arrows in his right talon, and a sprig of olive in his left. The scroll in his beak extends from over the right wing to the back of the left and bears the motto E PLURIBUS UNUM. Six cloud puffs embay thirteen stars above the eagle's head and the issuing authority, UNITED STATES OF AMERICA, involves the device. The denomination 25c is in the base, divided between the numeral "5" and the letter c by the eagle's tail. The border is denticled.

QUARTER DOLLAR (LIBERTY CAP WITH MOTTO), 1815-1828

Specifics

U.S. Coin No: 54
Type: III Quarter Dollar
Size: 18 or 1⅛" 1815
     17 or 1¹⁄₁₆" 1818-1828
Weight: 104 grains
Edge: Reeded

Composition: 892.4 silver,
    107.6 copper
Quantity minted: 1,274,581
Proofs minted: None of record
Mint marks: None
Designer: John Reich

Description

Obverse: A more buxom Liberty faces left. A tuft of hair protrudes from the lead edge of the Phrygian cap that is inscribed with the word LIBERTY, and an excessive amount of tresses extend below the shoulder and scroll under the shoulder line. Seven six-point stars are in radius in the border on the left with six in the border on the right. The date is in the base.

Reverse: An eagle displayed with inverted wings is positioned below center. In his right talon he holds a branch of olive, and in his left, three broadhead arrows. An arched scroll high above the eagle bears the motto E PLURIBUS UNUM. The issuing authority parallels the border from the right wing tip to the head of the first arrow and the denomination 25c is in exergue below the eagle. The border pattern is engrailed.

QUARTER DOLLAR (LIBERTY CAP/WITHOUT MOTTO), 1831-1838

Specifics

U.S. Coin No: 55
Type: IV Quarter Dollar
Size: 15 or 15⁄16″
Weight: 104 grains
Edge: Reeded

Composition: 892.4 silver,
107.6 copper
Quantity minted: 4,668,400
Proofs minted: Rare
Mint marks: None
Designer: William Kneass

Description

Obverse: The image of Liberty, facing left, is similar to, but noticeably different from the previous type. She is less buxom and fills a greater vertical area than her predecessor. Her hair is equally scrolled but less bulky. The stars on this coin are smaller but there are seven in radius on the left and six in radius on the right. Smaller numerals make up the date.

Reverse: A larger and slightly different eagle is positioned higher in the field. The Union shield on his breast is not on as radical an angle but his attitude is unchanged. In his left talon he holds three broad-head arrows, and in his right, a branch of olive.

The arched scroll bearing the motto has been omitted, and the issuing authority, UNITED STATES OF AMERICA, appears in much smaller type around the inner border. Below the eagle the denomination 25c is expressed.

This coin is smaller in diameter but correspondingly thicker than Type III.

QUARTER DOLLAR (LIBERTY SEATED), 1838-1866

Specifics

U.S. Coin No: 56
Type: V Quarter Dollar
Size: 15 or $^{15}/_{16}$″
Weight: 103½ grains to 1853.
Edge: Reeded

Composition: 90% silver,
    10% copper
Quantity minted: 54, 016,380
Proofs minted: 3,920
Mint marks: o and s
Designer: Christian Gobrecht

Description

Obverse: Gobrecht's Seated Liberty is the main device. In her left hand she holds a staff topped with the Phrygian cap. In her right hand she grasps a scroll bearing the word LIBERTY while supporting a Union shield. The scroll crosses the shield and turns back and under the sinister base.

Thirteen small six-point stars form an interrupted arc from the edge of the rock on the left to a point short of the foot on the right. The date is in the base.

Reverse: An eagle displayed with inverted wings shows a shield of the Union on his breast. An olive branch extends from his right talon and three arrows from his left. From the tip of the right wing around to the tip of the head of the arrow, the issuing authority, UNITED STATES OF AMERICA runs close to the inner border. The denomination QUAR. DOL. is expressed in this abbreviated form rather than in numerals.

QUARTER DOLLAR (LIBERTY SEATED), 1853

Specifics

U.S. Coin No: 57
Type: VI Quarter Dollar
Size: 15 or $^{15}\!/_{16}''$
Weight: 96 grains
Edge: Reeded

Composition: 90% silver,
    10% copper
Quantity minted: 16,586,220
Proofs minted: Rare
Mint marks: o-only
Designer: Christian Gobrecht

Description

Obverse: A reduction in the weight of the Liberty Seated Quarter Dollar was authorized by the Act of February 21, 1853. This reduction was indicated by two arrow heads at the date. Other than that, the designs for the Type V and the Type VI are identical.

Reverse: The authorization for the weight reduction also affected the reverse design in that it provided for a series of rays, reaching out from the center to the letter line of the issuing authority, UNITED STATES OF AMERICA. The rays were removed before the 1854 issue was struck, but the arrows at the date remained until 1856.

Note: Arrows at the date of any coin indicate a change in the weight but do not necessarily mean a reduction. They have been used to show an increase, as in the case of our next coin. Consider this when authenticating and also that arrows have been removed to create an unusual coin.

QUARTER DOLLAR (LIBERTY SEATED), 1866-1891

Specifics

U.S. Coin No: 58
Type: VII Quarter Dollar
Size: 15 or ¹⁵⁄₁₆″
Weight: 96 grains 1866-1873
       96.45 grains 1873-1965
Edge: Reeded

Composition: 90% silver,
      10% copper
Quantity minted: 75,014,816
Proofs minted: 21,313
Mint marks: o, s, and cc
Designer: Robert Ball Hughes

Description

Obverse: Liberty, the date, and the arrangement of the thirteen stars appear relatively unchanged from the previous type. The weight was increased by the Act of February 12, 1873, and this increase was indicated with arrows similar to those showing reduction. They were removed in 1875.

Reverse: The process of changing the weight did not affect the reverse design. The absence of the motto IN GOD WE TRUST from the three previous types was noted and rectified on this issue by adding a scrolled ribbon bearing that motto to the area above the head of the eagle. The motto E PLURIBUS UNUM did not appear from the time of the issuance of the Type V to the Type VIII Quarter Dollar.

The mint letters are located under the apex formed by the stem of the olive branch and the arrow feather.

QUARTER DOLLAR (LIBERTY HEAD), 1892-1916

Specifics

U.S. Coin No: 59
Type: VIII Quarter Dollar
Size: 15 or ¹⁵⁄₁₆″
Weight: 96.45 grains
Edge: Reeded

Composition: 90% silver,
10% copper
Quantity minted: 264,286,491
Proofs minted: 17,299
Mint marks: o, s, and d
Designer: Charles E. Barber

Description

Obverse: Liberty, wearing a combination laurel and slave's cap, faces right. Across the protruding hair runs a small band, inscribed LIBERTY. In radius above the head is the motto IN GOD WE TRUST. Six six-point stars flank the device on the left, and seven, on the right. The date is in radius in the base.

Reverse: An eagle is displayed with a Union shield on his breast. A scroll in his beak is inscribed with the motto E PLURIBUS UNUM. In his left talon he holds a bundle of thirteen arrows, and in his right an olive branch. Two dots separate the denomination QUARTER DOLLAR from the inscription of the issuing authority, UNITED STATES OF AMERICA, encircling the entire device. In 1892 the first five-point stars appeared on United States coins to make up the constellation of thirteen stars above the eagle's head. The mint marks are located below the eagle.

QUARTER DOLLAR (STANDING LIBERTY), 1916-1917

Specifics

U.S. Coin No: 60
Type: IX Quarter Dollar
Size: 15 or ¹⁵⁄₁₆″
Weight: 96.45 grains
Edge: Reeded

Composition: 90% silver,
10% copper
Quantity minted: 12,305,200
Proofs minted: None of record
Mint marks: D and S
Designer: Hermon A. MacNeil

Description

Obverse: A partially nude figure of MacNeil's Standing Liberty, holding an olive sprig in its extended right hand and the end of a shroud drawn from an armored shield on its left arm, stands on the first and second steps of a passway. On the left wall are the words IN GOD and a vertical pattern of seven five-point stars; on the right wall, the words WE TRUST over a vertical pattern of six stars. The word LIBERTY is in the legend with the L all but covered by the olive sprig. On the step the date is inscribed in relief. The border is the most unusual reel and bead of Greek and Roman architecture.

Reverse: A volant eagle in free flight from left to right is flanked on the left by seven five-point stars and on the right by six. UNITED STATES is in radius above, with the word OF separating the legend from AMERICA, below which runs the motto E PLURIBUS UNUM, in two lines. The denomination QUARTER DOLLAR is under the eagle, parallel with the plain border.

160

QUARTER DOLLAR (STANDING LIBERTY), 1917-1930

Specifics

U.S. Coin No: 61
Type: X Quarter Dollar
Size: 15 or $^{15}/_{16}''$
Weight: 96.45 grains
Edge: Reeded

Composition: 90% silver,
    10% copper
Quantity minted: 212,516,800
Proofs minted: None of record
Mint marks: D and S
Designer: Hermon A. MacNeil

Description

Obverse: Public reaction to the nudity of Liberty lead to a series of excuses for the production halt in early 1917, chief among them upgrading the general artistic merits of the eagle, which had also been publicly rejected.

When production of this Quarter Dollar was resumed in late 1917, the eagle had been repositioned closer to the center of the reverse and Liberty was clothed in a chain-mail slipover and a new hairdo.

The date in relief on the first step of the passway wore quickly and in 1925 the date area was recessed as an exergue to protect the relief. The reel-and-bead border pattern was retained.

MacNeil's initial M is to the right of the last star in the right-hand pattern on the obverse. Mint letters stand to the right of the last star in the left-hand pattern.

About the Model

Hermon MacNeil chose as his model petite Miss Dora Doscher, a five-foot-four-inch beauty. Her almost perfect dimensions were duplicated by Karl Bitter when he sculpted the famous "Diana" that reposes in the Metropolitan Museum of Art, and again, for the figure that surmounts the Pulitzer Memorial Fountain at 58th Street and Fifth Avenue in New York City.

Twenty-two-year old Dora had many intellectual and artistic pursuits—writer, lecturer, nurse—but her greatest accomplishment was her modeling career which she succeeded in despite her semi-invalidism as a child.

The Eagle

Some nationally known ornithologists considered this likeness of Peter, the mint eagle, an insult to that famous bird. They maintained it had the head of a hawk, the wings of an eagle, and the body of a dove.

Mint Letters and Designer's Initial.

The right-hand half of the illustration shows the actual location of Mr. MacNeil's initial м.

The left-hand half shows the mint letter location.

QUARTER DOLLAR (WASHINGTON HEAD/SILVER),
1932-1964

Specifics

U.S. Coin No: 62
Type: XI Quarter Dollar
Size: 15 or $^{15}/_{16}''$
Weight: 96.45 grains
Edge: Reeded

Composition: 90% silver,
10% copper
Quantity minted: 2,044,710,652
Proofs minted: 19,905,612
Mint marks: D and S
Designer: John Flanagan

Description

Obverse: To commemorate the two-hundredth anniversary of Washington's birth, a special Act of Congress dated March 4, 1931, authorized the issuance of the Washington Quarter Dollar. It replaced the Type X Standing Liberty, which had not been issued since 1930 and had served only fifteen years of its required twenty-five years of legal service.

The commemorative coin that is not a commemorative contains the bust of General Washington facing left with the motto IN GOD WE TRUST under the chin; the word LIBERTY is in radius in the legend. The date stands below.

Reverse: An eagle displayed with inverted wings, standing on a fasces of arrows pointing to the left. The issuing authority, UNITED STATES OF AMERICA, and the denomination QUARTER DOLLAR radius the legend and the base; the motto E PLURIBUS UNUM, in two lines, curves with the legend above the eagle, and below, two laurel branches curve with the denomination.

163

QUARTER DOLLAR (WASHINGTON HEAD/CLAD), 1965-date

Specifics

U.S. Coin No: 63
Type: XII Quarter Dollar
Size: 15 or $^{15}\!/_{16}''$
Weight: 87.5 grains
Edge: Reeded

Composition: Core—solid copper
    Clad—75% copper, 25% nickel
Quantity minted: 5,331,461,752*
Proofs minted: 8,608,950*
Mint marks: D (S Proofs only)
Designer: John Flanagan

Description

The Act of July 3, 1965, provided for the minting of a quarter dollar or twenty-five-cent piece composed of an alloy of 75% copper and 25% nickel clad on a core of pure copper. The clad quarter weighs 5.67 grams, or 9.3% less than the silver piece of the same denomination.

Section 3 of the act provides for specific recognition of the new coinage as legal tender of the United States.

*To 1970

Edge of Clad Quarter Dollar

About the Model

The likeness on this coin is General Washington's four years before he became President. It was modeled from the famous bust created by sculptor Jean-Antoine Houdon during his visit to Mount Vernon in 1785.

The bust was made at the insistence of the Virginia legislature, which resolved that measures be taken to procure a statue of the general in the finest marble and workmanship.

Benjamin Franklin, our ambassador to France, arranged for Houdon to come to America to accept the commission.

General Washington recorded the arrival of Houdon in this manner: "Sunday, October 2, 1785; After we were in bed, about 11 o'clock in the evening, Mr. Houdon, sent from France by Doctor Franklin and Mr. Jefferson to take my bust, in behalf of the State of Virginia, with three young assistants, introduced by a French Gentleman from Alexandria, arrived here by water from the latter place."

The Numismatist

About the Designer

Sculptor John Flanagan, the coin's designer, was the second to put the fasces on a general-circulation coin of the United States. The bundle of arrows bound with a ribbon is a stylized version of the Roman symbol of authority—a bundle of sticks, with a battle-ax in the center, bound with a red band.

Mr. Flanagan's initials, JF, may be found on the truncation of the neck.

HALF-DOLLAR (FLOWING HAIR), 1794-1795

Specifics

U.S. Coin No: 64
Type: I Half Dollar
Size: 21 or 1⅚₆"
Weight: 208 grains
Edge: Lettered

Composition: 892.4 silver
107.6 copper
Quantity minted: 323,144
Proofs minted: None of record
Mint marks: None
Designers: Robert Scot or
John Gardner

Description

Obverse: Coinage of the Half-Dollar was authorized by the Act of April 2, 1792, which established its weight and fineness in silver. The obverse design can be credited to Robert Scot or John Smith Gardner as both produced devices for the first Half-Dollar.

The well-groomed head of Liberty faces right. Shoulder-length tresses flow down and back. The upper tufts are contained without the aid of a fillet. The word LIBERTY is in the legend and the date appears below the scrolled truncation of the neck. Eight six-point stars and seven six-point stars are in radius at the inner border between the date and the legend on the left and right respectively.

Reverse: A fledgling eagle displayed with inverted wings occupies the area within a wreath of two laurel branches tied at the stem by a bowless knot. The issuing authority, UNITED STATES OF AMERICA, encircles the device. The border pattern is an extended denticle.

HALF-DOLLAR (DRAPED BUST/SE), 1796-1797

Specifics

U.S. Coin No: 65
Type: II Half-Dollar
Size: 21 or 1⁵⁄₁₆″
Weight: 208 grains
Edge: Lettered

Composition: 892.4 silver,
107.6 copper
Quantity minted: 3,918
Proofs minted: None of record
Mint marks: None
Designer: Robert Scot

Description

Obverse: Scot's buxom Liberty faces right, with shoulder-length tresses scrolled under at the shoulder line and almost touching the first digit in the date and the last star on the left. The temple strands are swept back and contained by a small multi-bowed ribbon. Shorter tufts lie forward on the brow. Fifteen six-point stars are arranged in an eight- and seven-pattern radius on the left and right borders respectively. LIBERTY appears in the legend, and the date, in the base.

Reverse: A fledgling eagle similar to the previous type but with his right wing drawn closer to his body, stands on a mound inside a wreath formed by a branch of laurel on the left and a palm branch on the right, tied by a ribbon and double bow. The issuing authority is in radius around the device, and the denomination, expressed in the fraction ½, under the wreath. The border pattern is an extended denticle.

HALF-DOLLAR (DRAPED BUST/HE), 1801-1806

Specifics

U.S. Coin No: 66
Type: III Half-Dollar
Size: 21 or 1⅝₁₆″
Weight: 208 grains
Edge: Lettered

Composition: 892.4 silver,
107.6 copper
Quantity minted: 1,444,268
Proofs minted: None of record
Mint marks: None
Designer: Robert Scot

Description

Obverse: The Liberty on this coin is not unlike that on the previous type II. The stars vary in size but not in arrangement and the word LIBERTY is erratically spaced on several specimens. Some dates indicate the use of hand-tooled numeral punches, which was almost a necessity in the preparation of early dies.

Reverse: A heraldic-eagle device with the eagle displayed holding in his beak a scroll inscribed with the motto E PLURIBUS UNUM. There is a Union shield on his breast, thirteen arrows in his right talon and a sprig of olive in his left. The inscription around the legend, UNITED STATES OF AMERICA, starts and ends at each of the eagle's claws. A constellation of thirteen six-point stars are embayed by six cloud puffs arched from the right to left wings. The only suggestion of the denomination is in the lettered edge, which reads FIFTY CENTS OR HALF A DOLLAR.

HALF-DOLLAR (LIBERTY CAP), 1807-1836

Specifics

U.S. Coin No: 67
Type: IV Half-Dollar
Size: 21 or 1⁵⁄₁₆″
Weight: 208 grains
Edge: Lettered

Composition: 892.4 silver,
      107.6 copper
Quantity minted: 82,293,204
Proofs minted: None of record
Mint marks: None
Designer: John Reich

Description

Obverse: The matronly head of Reich's Liberty facing left wears the slave's cap symbolic of Liberty. Small tufts of hair protrude from the edge of the cap, and excessive tresses extend below the shoulder line and end in a scroll above the last digit in the date. Six-point stars, seven at the left and six at the right, are in radius at the border. The required expression, LIBERTY, is inscribed on the cap, and the date is letter-spaced in the base.

Reverse: A disproportionate eagle low in the field is displayed with inverted wings and grasping an olive branch in the right talon and three broadhead arrows in the left. An angular Union shield is suspended on his breast. The legend in radius from left to right reads UNITED STATES OF AMERICA, and a scroll imprinted with E PLURIBUS UNUM parallels the legend. Below the eagle is the denomination, 50c.

The lettered edge reads FIFTY CENTS OR HALF DOLLAR.

HALF-DOLLAR (LIBERTY CAP), 1836-1837

Specifics

U.S. Coin No: 68
Type: V Half-Dollar
Size: 19 or 1¾₆″
Weight: 206¼ grains

Edge: Reeded

Composition: 90% silver,
    10% copper

Quantity minted:
    1836: Incl. in Type IV
    1837: 3,629,820
Proofs minted: Rare
Mint marks: None
Designer: Christian Gobrecht

Description

Obverse: The motif in this design is similar to the preceding one except that the profile of Liberty is decidedly Roman. Small six-point stars spaced on a wider index still radius the right and left borders, but the quantity in each pattern is reversed. This type shows six on the left and seven on the right. The date is in the base but the numerals are confined and much smaller. LIBERTY is inscribed on the band of the cap.

Reverse: A similar, but noticeably different, eagle with inverted wings closer in holds three broad-head arrows in his left talon and a sprig of olive in his right. UNITED STATES OF AMERICA parallels the radius of the upper border but the scroll and motto have been omitted. The denomination 50 cents is in the base.

HALF-DOLLAR (LIBERTY CAP), 1838-1839

Specifics

U.S. Coin No: 69
Type: VI Half-Dollar
Size: 19 or 1 3/16"
Weight: 206 1/4 grains
Edge: Reeded

Composition: 90% silver,
     10% copper
Quantity minted: 7,043,556
Proofs minted: Rare
Mint marks: o only
Designer: Christian Gobrecht

Description

Obverse: Close observation will disclose a difference in the Liberty on this coin and the one on the previous type. The facial-configuration lines show a recess at the brow line that reduces the Roman appearance. Otherwise, the devices on Type V and VI are the same.

Reverse: Like the obverse device, the eagle is similar in nature to that of Type V, but on closer examination, it differs greatly in fine details—enough, at least, to be considered in authentication.

The arrow heads and the olive-branch leaves are smaller. The type face in the issuing authority is more accurately spaced, and in the base, HALF DOL. replaces the 50 cents as denomination.

The borders on both sides for Type V and Type VI are of the embattlement type.

The first mint mark appeared on the 1838 Half-Dollar. An o for the New Orleans Branch Mint was affixed to the obverse between the drape folds and the date.

HALF-DOLLAR (LIBERTY SEATED), 1839-1866

Specifics

U.S. Coin No: 70
Type: VII Half-Dollar
Size: 19 or 1¾₆″
Weight: 206¼ grains 1839-1853
          192 grains 1853-1866
Edge: Reeded

Composition: 90% silver,
          10% copper
Quantity minted: 90,326,651
Proofs minted: 2,980
Mint marks: o and s
Designer: Christian Gobrecht

Description

Obverse: Liberty Seated is facing left. In her left hand she holds a staff topped by the Phrygian slave's cap symbolic of Liberty, and in her right hand, bracing a Union shield, she grasps a scroll that runs diagonally across the shield to its sinister base and turns under. Inscribed on the scroll is the word LIBERTY.

Liberty's loose-fitting robe, held by shoulder straps, extends to the base of the device and scrolls over her left leg, thrust to a point at the border. Thirteen small six-point stars arc the device from the protruding edge of the rock to within one index space of Liberty's foot.

The eagle displayed is not unlike the eagle on Type VI. The issuing authority, UNITED STATES OF AMERICA, is inscribed in the legend. The denomination reads HALF. DOL.

HALF-DOLLAR (LIBERTY SEATED), 1853

Specifics

U.S. Coin No: 71
Type: VIII Half-Dollar
Size: 19 or 1³⁄₁₆″
Weight: 192 grains
Edge: Reeded

Composition: 90% silver,
10% copper
Quantity minted: 4,960,708
Proofs minted: None
Mint marks: o only
Designer: Christian Gobrecht

Description

Obverse: The weight of this Half-Dollar was authorized reduced by the Act of February 21, 1853, and arrows at the date indicate that reduction. Other than that, there is no appreciable difference between the Type VII and the Type VIII obverse.

Reverse: The authorization for the weight reduction also affected the reverse design, which remained the same as in the previous issue except for a series of rays reaching out from the center to the lower letter line of the issuing authority, UNITED STATES OF AMERICA, and to the upper letter line of the denomination HALF DOL. in the base.

The rays were removed for the 1854 issue, but the arrows remained until the completion of the 1855 issue.

Note: As mentioned before, arrows at the date indicate a change in weight but not necessarily a reduction. They have also been used to show an increase and have been removed to create an unusual coin.

HALF-DOLLAR (LIBERTY SEATED), 1866-1891

Specifics

U.S. Coin No: 72
Type: IX Half-Dollar
Size: 19 or 1¾₁₆″
Weight: 192 grains 1866-1872
      192.9 grains 1873-1965
Edge: Reeded

Composition: 90% silver,
    10% copper
Quantity minted: 61,395,551
Proofs minted: 20,873
Mint marks: s and cc
Designer: Christian Gobrecht

Description

Obverse: There is a slight difference between the Gobrecht device on this coin and that on the previous type. Since the staff held by Liberty is shorter from the hand to the tip, there is less space between the finger of the right hand and the edge of the cap. This is a small matter but one to consider when authenticating. Other than that, the obverse of U.S. Coin No. 72 is like that of Coin No. 70. The stars are indexed the same but appear larger and closer to the border on this piece.

Reverse: The reverse is not unlike that of the preceding type, except for a reduction in the size of the eagle to provide space for a scroll that arches above the eagle and bears the motto IN GOD WE TRUST.

The mint letters are located below the eagle.

HALF-DOLLAR (LIBERTY HEAD), 1892-1915

Specifics

U.S. Coin No: 73
Type: X Half-Dollar
Size: 19 or 1¾₁₆″
Weight: 192.9 grains
Edge: Reeded

Composition: 90% silver, 10% copper
Quantity minted: 142,843,922
Proofs minted: 17,313
Mint marks: o, s, and D
Designer: Charles E. Barber

Description

Obverse: Liberty, wearing a combination laurel and slave's cap, faces right. A small band across the protruding hair is inscribed LIBERTY. In radius above the head is the motto IN GOD WE TRUST. Thirteen six-point stars flank the device—six on the left and seven on the right. The date is in the base.

Reverse: A displayed eagle with a Union shield on his breast holds thirteen arrows in his left talon and a branch of olive in his right. A scroll in his beak is inscribed with the motto E PLURIBUS UNUM. The issuing authority, UNITED STATES OF AMERICA, and the denomination HALF DOLLAR, separated by a dot before and after each expression, completely encircle the device. The first five-point stars to appear as a symbol on a United States coin form a thirteen-star constellation above the eagle's head. Barber's initial B may be found on the latter portion of the truncation of the neck.

HALF-DOLLAR (WALKING LIBERTY), 1916-1947

Specifics

U.S. Coin No: 74
Type: XI Half-Dollar
Size: 19 or 1¾₆"
Weight: 192.9 grains
Edge: Reeded

Composition: 90% silver,
10% copper
Quantity minted: 485,478,441
Proofs minted: 74,400
Mint marks: D and S
Designer: Adolph A. Weinman

Description

Obverse: Liberty, dressed in a garment representing the flag of the United States, appears to be walking left. Her right leg extends backward and her right arm, forward. She is wearing the traditional Phrygian cap and in her left arm bears branches of laurel and oak. Several five-point stars are visible in the upper cape-like portion of her dress. The striped quarter below the extended arm scrolls over the fifth and sixth rays of the sun in the lower foreground. LIBERTY is letterspaced in the legend; the motto IN GOD WE TRUST is double-lined below the letter Y; and the date is on the base.

Reverse: An American bald eagle, perched on a mountain ledge with his wings inverted, thrusts his right talon forward on a pine sapling. The inscription UNITED STATES OF AMERICA is in radius above and HALF DOLLAR appears in the base. E PLURIBUS UNUM is double-lined above the pine sapling.

176

This is the first coin since the Half-Dollar of 1838 (U.S. Coin No. 69) that a mint letter has appeared on the obverse. In 1916 the letters for Denver and San Francisco were placed under the motto IN GOD WE TRUST in the lower right-hand quarter of the coin. In 1917 they again appeared both on the obverse and the reverse, creating two major varieties.

The reverse location for the mint mark is forward of the ledge, under the pine sapling in the lower left quarter of the coin.

Designer's Initial.

Adolph A. Weinman was a meticulous person and was one of the few designers to apply his monogram in an artistic manner. Others who did so were Augustus Saint-Gaudens, designer of the Double Eagle, Anthony de Francisci, designer of the Peace Dollar, and Gilroy Roberts, designer of the Kennedy Half-Dollar.

Mr. Weinman's monogram is located at the opposite end of the ledge on which the eagle is standing, and just under the wing tip in the lower right-hand quarter of the reverse.

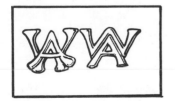

Its true construction is discernible with a magnifying glass.

The monogram is read A under A over W. His initials on the Dime of 1916 (U.S. Coin No. 48) are A under W.

HALF-DOLLAR (FRANKLIN HEAD), 1948-1963

Specifics

U.S. Coin No: 75
Type: XII Half-Dollar
Size: 19 or 1¾₆″
Weight: 192.9 grains
Edge: Reeded

Composition: 90% silver,
10% copper
Quantity minted: 481,801,407
Proofs minted: 15,886,955
Mint marks: D and S
Designer: John R. Sinnock

Description

Obverse: The head of Benjamin Franklin, facing right, more than dominates the field of the obverse. The word LIBERTY appears in the legend and the motto IN GOD WE TRUST is in radius at the bottom. The date is below the chin and toward the letter T in TRUST.

Reverse: Here again the device occupies more than its proportionate share of the field. An extremely accurate reproduction of the Liberty Bell with its wood belfry reaches the letter lines of UNITED STATES OF AMERICA in radius above and the denomination HALF DOLLAR in radius in the base. To the left the motto E PLURIBUS UNUM is set in three lines and to the right an eagle displayed.

The Franklin Half-Dollar had served only fifteen of the required twenty-five years service when it was discontinued in response to a special Act of Congress that replaced it with the Kennedy Half-Dollar. The initials, JRS, for designer John R. Sinnock, are at the latter portion of the neck truncation.

The Franklin Model

Mr. Sinnock modeled the Franklin bust from the original by Jean-Antoine Houdon, the sculptor who created the General Washington bust.

The work was done from life during Doctor Franklin's tenure as ambassador to France, and just prior to Houdon's visit to the United States.

The Small Eagle

The records show that Franklin opposed the use of heads of any kind on currency. He believed that the space should be devoted to proverbs of thrift.

Doctor Franklin also opposed the eagle as an emblem of the United States, and denounced it as a coward and bird of prey. He suggested the turkey as more worthy of the honor.

The coinage law requires an eagle on the reverse of a Half-Dollar and Gilroy Roberts, who designed the eagle, tried to respect Mr. Franklin's wishes by making it as small as possible.

A "Commercial"

The Franklin Half-Dollar is the only U.S. coin to legally carry the name of a private firm.

When the Liberty Bell was damaged in shipment, it was repaired by the firm of Pass and Stow. Their name appears at the apex of the crack in the bell by a resolution of the Philadelphia Assembly, who ordered it cast as a courtesy to the craftsmen that repaired it.

HALF-DOLLAR (KENNEDY HEAD/SILVER), 1964

Specifics

U.S. Coin No: 76
Type: XIII Half-Dollar
Size: 19 or 1¾₁₆″
Weight: 192.9 grains
Edge: Reeded

Composition: 90% silver,
           10% copper
Quantity minted: 433,460,212
Proofs minted: 3,950,762
Mint marks: D only
Designers: Obverse, Gilroy Roberts
           Reverse, Frank Gasparro

Description

Obverse: The device is the likeness of President John F. Kennedy, facing left. It rises higher on the field than the average, causing the hair to partially cover the letters B, E, and R in the word LIBERTY which is letterspaced in the legend. Also letterspaced in the base is the date, 1964. The motto IN GOD WE TRUST is divided. The first two words are positioned to the left of the point of the neck, and the last two words repose on the same plane to the right of the neck line.

Reverse: The seal of the President of the United States is well defined in the field. A Union shield rests on the breast of an eagle displayed, which holds an olive branch in the right talon and thirteen arrows in the left. A scroll in the eagle's beak bears the motto E PLURIBUS UNUM, and rays originating from the center penetrate a constellation of thirteen stars and thirteen cloud puffs. An amulet of fifty stars encloses the device surrounded by UNITED STATES OF AMERICA and HALF DOLLAR.

The Designer's Initials

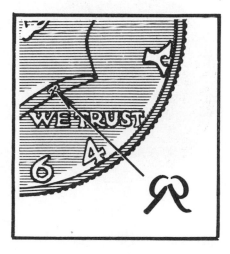

Gilroy Roberts

The obverse device was designed by Gilroy Roberts as Chief Engraver of the United States Mint at Philadelphia.

His initials, GR, located on the truncation of the neck, are one of the three artistic monograms used by designers of United States coins.

The stylized G and R were the subject of concern among many who chose to describe them as a device of a political belief contrary to that of the United States. This is one of the hazards of being artistic.

(See Chapter V, *How United States Coins Are Made,* for the process used to produce the Kennedy Half-Dollar.)

Frank Gasparro

Mr. Gasparro designed the reverse of the Kennedy Half-Dollar with as much concern for his subject matter as Mr. Roberts. Neither design is overdone nor artificial in concept. Mr. Gasparro realized that President Kennedy liked the Presidential Seal and he exerted every effort to do the work justice. His initials, FG, are slightly monogrammed and appear at the apex of the left leg and the last tail feather.

The same initials are found on the reverse of the Lincoln Memorial One-Cent reverse. Gasparro is the first designer to have his signature on the same coin with other designers.

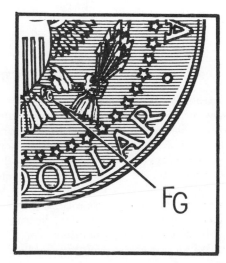

HALF-DOLLAR (Kennedy Head/Silver Clad), 1965–1970

Specifics

U.S. Coin No: 77
Type: XIV Half-Dollar
Size: 19 or 1³⁄₁₆″
Weight: 177.5 grains
Edge: Reeded

Composition:
  Core: 40% silver, 60% copper
  Clad: 80% silver, 20% copper
Quantity minted:
  848,895,006
Proofs Minted: 8,608,950
Mint marks: D (S proofs only)
Designers: Gilroy Roberts
           Frank Gasparro

Description

Obverse: The Coinage Act of June, 1965, authorized the minting of a new series of coins in the denominations of 10, 25, and 50 cents. In the case of the 50-cent piece, the outside, or cladding, layers would be composed of an alloy of 80 percent silver and 20 percent copper and the core of a silver-copper alloy of such fineness that the overall composition of each coin would be 40 percent silver and 60 percent copper.

Section 9 of the act empowered the secretary of the treasury to mint coins bearing the date of issuance, or, if in the judgment of the secretary, this would cause a coin shortage, he may direct that new coinage be marked with the date of the preceding year. Counterfeiting laws apply to the cupro-nickel and silver-clad coinage.

The Location of the Mint Letter

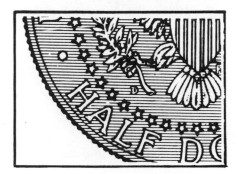

The 1964 issue of the new Kennedy Half-Dollar was struck at both the Philadelphia and Denver mints, but only the mint letter D is shown. It is located on the reverse under the eagle's right talon, which holds the olive branch.

The initials, FG, for Frank Gasparro, the designer of the reverse, are in the apex of the left leg and the last tail feather.

Due to an emergency control measure applied by the Bureau of the Mint, Kennedy Half-Dollars for the years 1965, 1966, and 1967 bore no indication of their point of origin. This measure, intended to keep the new halves in circulation, reduced the possibilities of speculation insofar as the mint source was concerned. It did not, however, prevent the Half-Dollar from being withheld by both the speculator and the memento collector.

In 1968 the Kennedy Half-Dollar became the third coin of that denomination to bear a mint mark on its obverse. Other such coins were the Half-Dollar of 1838 (U.S. Coin No. 69) and the Half-Dollar of 1916 (U.S. Coin No. 74).

This was a Bureau of the Mint directive and not a provision of the new coinage law.

The mint letter D on general-circulation coinage and the letter s on proof coins will be found in the field just under the forward point of the neck truncation.

HALF-DOLLAR (KENNEDY HEAD/CLAD), 1971 to date

Specifics

U.S. Coin No: 117
Type: XV Half-Dollar
Size: 19 or 1-3/16"
Weight: 175.0 grains
Edge: Reeded

Composition: Core: pure copper
           Clad: 75% copper, 25% nickel
Quantity minted: 457,261,424—1971
Proofs minted: 3,224,138—1971
Mint marks: D (S proofs only)
Designers: Gilroy Roberts
           Frank Gasparro

Description

Obverse: The Coinage Act of June 1965 was amended in part by the act of November 5, 1970 (see pp. 68 and 69 for both acts) to provide for the discontinuance of silver in the Kennedy Half-Dollar. Since the design may not change until completion of its 25-year service period, it remained the same as previous issues.

The alloy for the 1971 Half-Dollar denomination was changed in accordance with paragraph (*b*) Section 201 of the new act which read: "(*b*) Any coin minted under the authority of sub-section (*a*) shall be a clad coin. The cladding shall be an alloy of 75 percentum copper and 25 percentum nickel, and shall weigh not less than 30 percentum of the weight of the whole coin. The core shall be copper."

Edge: Although it is possible to see the alloyed core in the "silver clad" issue of Kennedy Half-Dollars, it will be very noticeable beginning with the 1971 issue. Type XIV Kennedy Halves have been known to be deliberately silver plated outside the Mint facilities. Special note should be given to the Type XV, since plating creates the illusion that a 1971 Kennedy Half-dollar was mistakenly struck on a silver clad planchet.

The Three Kennedy Half-Dollars

When one design of an authorized coin is officially struck in two or more compositions their identity usually can be established by their dates. The 1943 steel cent and the 1944 bronze cent are good examples. However, for the purpose of creating a collectors' item, coins of one date and composition have been altered or plated to resemble a coin of one date accidentally struck on the planchet of another date.

Example: Kennedy Half-Dollars issued in 1964 were of a 90% silver alloy. Those struck from 1965 to 1970 had their composition changed to an alloy of less silver, and the 1971 issue contains no silver at all. If the second series from 1965 to 1970 suffered the indignities of being plated illegally, such a practice must be anticipated when the 1971 silverless Half-Dollar is released.

Caution: Examine any so-called Mint error closely by performing a specific gravity test as explained in Chapter XI in this book. Look at the valleys between the edge reedings. If the coin has been plated, a color will show, especially if scratched with a needle.

Kennedy Half-Dollar Edges

1964—Silver

1965—1970—Silver Clad

1971—Silverless

ONE DOLLAR (FLOWING HAIR), 1794-1795

Specifics

U.S. Coin No: 78
Type: I Dollar
Size: 24 or 1½"
Weight: 416 grains
Edge: Lettered

Composition: 892.4 silver,
      107.6 Copper
Quantity minted: 204,791
Proofs minted: Questionable
Mint marks: None
Designers: Robert Scot
      John Gardner

Description

Obverse: The attractive head of Liberty, with her hair flowing down and back without the aid of a fillet, is facing right. The scroll of the lowest tress barely touches the last star in the radius pattern of eight on the left. Above her runs the legend LIBERTY, and the date is in radius in the base. Seven stars curve parallel to the right border.

Edge: The edge is lettered HUNDRED CENTS, ONE DOLLAR OR UNIT, and unlike the lettered edge of a minor coin, this is a security measure in advance of the reeded edge.

Reverse: A small fledgling eagle displayed with inverted wings in the center area is surrounded by a wreath of two laurel branches tied by a bowless knot. The issuing authority, UNITED STATES OF AMERICA, encompasses the wreath and touches its leaves intermittently from the first letter U to the letter R. The border pattern is extended denticles.

ONE DOLLAR (DRAPED BUST/SMALL EAGLE), 1795-1798

Specifics

U.S. Coin No: 79
Type: II Dollar
Size: 24 or 1½"
Weight: 416 grains
Edge: Lettered

Composition: 892.4 silver,
107.6 copper
Quantity minted: 408,322
Proofs minted: None of record
Mint marks: None
Designer: Gilbert Stuart

Description

Obverse: With her hair partially confined at the back by ribbon, Liberty faces right. The lower scroll of her shoulder-length tresses touches the last star in the left-hand pattern of eight. Short tufts of hair on the top of Liberty's head reach into the letter line of LIBERTY in the legend. The date is in radius at the base.

Edge: The edge is lettered HUNDRED CENTS ONE DOLLAR OR UNIT.

Reverse: A small eagle, perched on a mound, his right wing drawn in closer to his body, occupies the area within a wreath formed by two half-wreaths of laurel and palm, crossed and tied at the stems by a ribbon and double bow. Here and there, the leaves are touched by letters in the inscription, UNITED STATES OF AMERICA. The border pattern is extended denticles.

ONE DOLLAR (DRAPED BUST/HERALDIC EAGLE), 1798-1803

Specifics

U.S. Coin No: 80
Type: III Dollar
Size: 25 or 1⅑₁₆"
Weight: 416 grains
Edge: Lettered

Composition: 892.4 silver
           107.6 copper
Quantity minted: 806,603
Proofs minted: Rare
Mint marks: None
Designer: Gilbert Stuart

Description

Obverse: The previous version of Liberty was retained on this type. The star pattern was changed to include seven on the left border and six on the right.

Edge: The edge is lettered HUNDRED CENTS ONE DOLLAR OR UNIT.

Reverse: The Great Seal of the United States definitely had some influence on this coin. The eagle displayed has a large Union shield on his breast, a scroll inscribed E PLURIBUS UNUM in his beak, thirteen arrows in his right talon, and an olive branch in his left. Six cloud puffs embay thirteen stars above the eagle's head, and the entire device is encompassed by the inscription UNITED STATES OF AMERICA.

Some varieties show only ten and twelve arrows, and some as many as fifteen stars in the constellation.

The Famous 1804 Silver Dollar

The 1804 Silver Dollar is one of the most mysterious pieces in the history of United States coinage. Officially, there are no dollars with this date. Those bearing the date 1804 are from two possible points of origin—inside or outside the United States Mint. Most are actually products of counterfeiters. The few struck with mint facilities, however, have been verified as antedated pieces (made after 1804).

Counterfeits, altered coins, and electrotypes of this "King of Coins" are known to exist and any specimen offered or exhibited should be supported by more than the normal pedigree.

Any further speculation would only add to the already overexercised controversy regarding its history.

Note: We recommend one highly respected work on this subject to the researcher: *The Fantastic 1804 Dollar,* by Eric P. Newman and Kenneth E. Bressett, Whitman Publishing Co., 1962, Library of Congress Catalog Card No. 62-19453.

ONE DOLLAR (CHRISTIAN GOBRECHT), 1836

Specifics

U.S. Coin No:	*Composition:* 90% silver,
Type: Specimen Dollar	10% copper
Edge: Plain and Reeded	*Quantity minted:* 1,026
	Proofs minted: 1,026
	Mint marks: None

Description

Production of the Silver Dollar was suspended in 1804 and resumed in 1840. During that period there were some changes in the coinage, and both Kneass and Goebrecht turned out new designs for the 1838 pattern Half-Dollar; but the Silver Dollar of 1836 was the work of Christian Gobrecht and served up as a specimen only.

Obverse: The seated figure of Liberty holds a staff topped by a Phrygian slave's cap in the left hand and a Union shield in the right together with the end of a scroll bearing the word LIBERTY. The scroll spans diagonally across the shield to the sinister base and turns under.

Mr. Gobrecht placed his name on the field under the plane on which Liberty is resting. It appears as C GOBRECHT F. (F. meaning *fecit,* or "made it" from the Latin word *facere,* meaning "to do" or "to make"). There were no further markings on the obverse.

The reverse has an eagle volant (in free flight) amidst a constellation of six-point stars in varied sizes. Around the design is the inscription UNITED STATES OF AMERICA.

ONE DOLLAR (LIBERTY SEATED), 1840-1866

Specifics

U.S. Coin No: 81
Type: IV Dollar
Size: 24 or 1½″
Weight: 412½ grains
Edge: Reeded

Composition: 90% silver,
10% copper
Quantity minted: 2,895,673
Proofs minted: 4,390
Mint marks: o and s
Designers: Christian Gobrecht
Robert Ball Hughes

Description

Obverse: Liberty, facing left, is seated on a rock and holds a staff topped by a Phrygian slave's cap. Her right hand supports the right tip of a Union shield and holds a scroll on which is inscribed LIBERTY. The shield is angled slightly from the center. Thirteen six-point stars circumscribe the device from left to right, interrupted between the seventh, eighth, and ninth by the head of Liberty and the slave's cap. The date is in the base.

Reverse: A displayed eagle with inverted wings and a Union shield on his breast holds an olive branch and three broad-head arrows in his right and left talons respectively. Over the device and parallel with the border is the inscription, UNITED STATES OF AMERICA. Below, in the base, is the denomination, ONE DOL.

ONE DOLLAR (LIBERTY SEATED), 1866-1873

Specifics

U.S. Coin No: 82
Type: V Dollar
Size: 24 or 1½"
Weight: 412¼ grains
Edge: Reeded

Composition: 90% silver,
    10% copper
Quantity minted: 3,603,948
Proofs minted: 6,060
Mint marks: s and cc
Designer: Robert Hughes after Christian Gobrecht

Description

Obverse: The Liberty Seated device for this type is not unlike the obverse design for Type IV. Its purpose was to soothe members of Congress who resented issue of the dollar or unit without the motto IN GOD WE TRUST.

Reverse: The figure of the eagle displayed was not disturbed, nor was the inscription UNITED STATES OF AMERICA, by the insertion of a scroll bearing the motto. The mint letters are located just under the eagle's right talon and the end of the olive branch.

The Silver Dollar was discontinued by the Act of February 12, 1873.

TRADE DOLLAR (LIBERTY SEATED), 1873-1885

Specifics

U.S. Coin No: 83
Type: VI Dollar
Size: 24 or 1½"
Weight: 420 grains
Edge: Reeded

Composition: 90% silver,
     10% copper
Quantity minted: 35,960,360
Proofs minted: 11,404
Mint marks: s and cc
Designer: William Barber

Description

The Trade Dollar, originally intended to circulate as a competitive trading medium with the Mexican dollar throughout the Orient, was in fact nothing more than an overweight subsidiary coin of the United States. Although it weighed more than the standard Dollar, it actually was turned down by some merchants or purchased for less than face value.

Obverse: The figure of Liberty, facing left, is seated on a bale of cotton with her right hand holding an olive sprig toward the open sea. To her back stands a sheaf of wheat, and in her left hand, she holds a scroll inscribed with the word LIBERTY. Thirteen stars encompass the device, and the date is in the base.

Reverse: An eagle displayed with inverted wings and three arrows in his right talon and an olive branch in his left. A scroll above his head reads E PLURIBUS UNUM, and below, in a radius not consistent with that of the coin, is the weight, 420 GRAINS; 900. FINE. TRADE DOLLAR is inscribed in the base and UNITED STATES OF AMERICA, in the legend.

ONE DOLLAR (LIBERTY HEAD/MORGAN), 1878-1904, 1921

Specifics

U.S. Coin No: 84
Type: VII Dollar
Size: 24 or 1½″
Weight: 412½ grains
Edge: Reeded

Composition: 90% silver,
10% copper
Quantity minted: 627,451,520
Proofs minted: 23,416
Mint marks: O, D, S, and CC
Designer: George Morgan

Description

The Bland-Allison Act of February 28, 1878, reinstated the domestic Silver Dollar with properties prescribed by the Act of January 18, 1937.

Liberty, facing left, wears a Phrygian cap ornate with a spray of wheat and cotton and a small fillet on the lead edge inscribed LIBERTY. Her tresses scroll around and forward on the neck truncation to the center of the date in the base. Seven small stars on the left and six on the right parallel the border to the motto E PLURIBUS UNUM in the legend.

Reverse: An eagle displayed holds an olive branch in his right talon and three arrows in his left. Two short branches of laurel tied with a double bow form a half-wreath that encloses the lower half of the eagle from the center of one wing to the center of the other.

IN GOD WE TRUST in Old English print is inscribed above the eagle, and the entire device is surrounded by UNITED STATES OF AMERICA and ONE DOLLAR. The border is denticled.

In God we trust

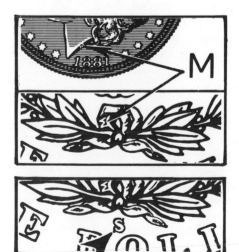

About the Model

Miss Anna Williams, an instructor of philosophy and methods in a school near the Philadelphia Mint, reluctantly posed for George Morgan's Liberty on the 1878 Silver Dollar.

Miss Williams refused Mr. Morgan's invitations to assist him in this project, but his persuasive manner was apparently stronger than Anna's modesty, and Mr. Morgan designed the device in five sittings with the Quaker City beauty.

It is still considered one of the finest pieces turned out by the Philadelphia facility.

George Morgan was formerly an engraver with the Royal Mint in London and his first assignment with the United States Mint was the reverse of the Silver Dollar.

The use of Old English in the motto above the eagle was the first appearance of this kind of lettering on a United States coin.

Mr. Morgan's initial M appears in two places on this coin. It is found at the tip of the hair scroll on the truncation of the neck, and again, on the reverse inside of the left loop of the bow, horizontal to the design.

Mint Marks

Any one of the letters O, D, S, or CC can be found under the apex of the ribbon ends of the bow on the reverse. The absence of a letter indicates a product of the Philadelphia Mint.

ONE DOLLAR (LIBERTY HEAD/PEACE), 1921-1935

Specifics

U.S. Coin No: 85
Type: VIII Peace Dollar
Size: 24 or 1½"
Weight: 412½" grains
Edge: Reeded

Composition: 90% silver,
10% copper
Quantity minted: 190,577,279
Proofs minted: None of record
Mint marks: D and S
Designer: Anthony DeFrancisci

Description

The Peace Dollar was issued to mark the termination of hostilities between the United States and Germany, and is the first coin ever minted to commemorate peace.

Obverse: The stylized version of the Statue of Liberty faces left. Radiants from her hair intrude into the word LIBERTY in the legend and partially obstruct the letter B. IN GOD WE TRVST is divided between WE and TRVST by the neck, which is truncated to a point touching the numeral "9" in the date.

Reverse: An eagle with folded wings grasps an olive branch. Perched on a ledge, he seems to be looking into the sun. The sun's rays radiate from a point at about five o'clock to all points in the field. The denomination ONE DOLLAR is inscribed through the rays.

UNITED STATES OF AMERICA and the motto E PLURIBUS UNUM parallel the upper border, and the word PEACE is in radius on the ledge.

About the Model

Teresa Cafarelli was a five-year-old immigrant girl from Italy when she got her first glimpse of the Statue of Liberty. From that day on, she lived the part of Liberty.

She talked about it incessantly to anyone who would listen and volunteered for all the school plays as long as she could portray the part of the famous statue.

Anthony DeFrancisci was also an Italian immigrant who had served his apprenticeship in the arts under such sculptors as Fraser, the designer of the Indian Head Nickel, and Adolph Weinman, designer of the Liberty Head Dime.

When DeFrancisci was thirty-three years old, he received his commission to design the new Peace Dollar to be issued in 1921, and since the task required a model, he decided to use his wife—Teresa Cafarelli.

Designer's Monogram

DeFrancisci's signature is one of the rare artistic monograms found on United States coins. The letter F superimposed over the letter A may be found on the field of the obverse above the last numeral in the date and below the neck of Liberty.

Mint Marks

Mint letters D or S are located on the reverse next to the border, above the eagle's tail and below the last sun ray on the left. The letter should be aligned vertically with the N in ONE.

ONE DOLLAR (EISENHOWER HEAD/SILVER CLAD)
1971–1972

Specifics

U.S. Coin No: 118
Type: IX Dollar
Size: 24 or 1½"
Weight: 379.47 grains
Edge: Reeded

Composition: 40.9 parts silver
59.1 parts copper
Quantity minted: 6,668,526—1971
Proofs minted: 1,222,170—1971
Mint marks: S—silver clad only
Designer: Frank Gasparro

Description

On November 5, 1969 the House of Representatives passed certain revisions to the Coinage Act of 1965 to allow the issuance of an Eisenhower Dollar coin. But the same bill did not pass the Senate until September 16, 1970, after which it became the current Coinage Act.

Paragraph (*d*) of Section 101 circumvented an earlier paragraph setting down specifications for the issuance of an all-clad coinage. It read in part: "Notwithstanding the foregoing, the Secretary is authorized to mint and issue not more than one hundred and fifty million one-dollar pieces which shall . . . [weigh] 24.592 grams and contain 9.837 grams of silver and 14.755 grams of copper."

This is the first one-dollar coin issued by the United States since 1935, and on completion of the approved 150,000,000 pieces with a silver content it represents the last silver coin in the United States circulating medium.

See Mr. Gasparro's comments regarding his design on page 199.

ONE DOLLAR (EISENHOWER HEAD/CLAD) 1971 to date

Specifics

U.S. Coin No: 119
Type: X Dollar
Size: 24 or 1½"
Weight: 349.997 Grains
Edge: Reeded

Composition: Core: copper
　　　　　　 Clad: 75% copper, 25% nickel
Quantity minted: 116,386,424—1971
Proofs minted: None in Cupro-nickel
Mint marks: D
Designer: Frank Gasparro

Description

Obverse: The strong features of the truncated Eisenhower profile reflects the character and determination of the late president. As a main device on the one-dollar coin it is arched by the inscription LIBERTY with the date radius in the base. The second motto IN GOD WE TRUST occupies an area in the field between seven and eight o'clock. Mint marks will be found below the neck truncation.

Reverse: The lettering on both sides of the new dollar is not unlike the lettering on the Peace Dollar of 1921–1935. An adaptation of the official insignia for Apollo XI serves as the reverse device with the first motto E PLURIBUS UNUM embayed above the eagle by an arched inscription of the issuing authority—UNITED STATES OF AMERICA. The denomination ONE DOLLAR is radius in the base.

Mr. Gasparro's signature FG may be found on the neck cutoff and at the apex of the eagle's center tail feather and the tip of the olive branch.

Obverse	Reverse

Comprehensive sketch

Flanged Galvanos

Finished coin

THE DEPARTMENT OF THE TREASURY

UNITED STATES MINT

PHILADELPHIA, PA. 19106

OFFICE OF THE
SUPERINTENDENT

November 16, 1971

Mr. F. Morton Reed
1572 Bellevue Drive,
Wooster, Ohio

Dear Mort:

I began collecting photographs of General Eisenhower
after seeing him in the 1945 Victory Parade. Later
on I executed and exhibited his portrait bust from a
study of those photographs.

When I was asked to create a design for the new dollar
it was as though I had been in training for a great
event. Having studied the subject well, my wax models
for the obverse portrait and the reverse eagle were
completed by November 1969.

Following a long delay in Congressional authorization
our red letter day arrived when President Nixon signed
the dollar bill into law. Meanwhile, my staff worked
diligently to bring up a pair of dies suitable for the
coins production.

When Mamie Eisenhower was shown the design, she liked
it very much - and we were on our way.

These and other experiences with the dollar were very
pleasant, but none would have been possible had the
Mint family not worked so hard as a team to bring it
to a reality.

With kindest personal regards,

Frank

Frank Gasparro
Chief Engraver

FG/ns

Keep Freedom in Your Future With U.S. Savings Bonds

CHAPTER VII

UNITED STATES GOLD COINS

Types of Gold Coins

One Dollar Gold	$1.00	Eagle	$10.00
Quarter Eagle	$2.50	Dougle Eagle	$20.00
Half Eagle	$5.00	Three Dollars	$3.00

Gold and the U.S. Monetary Standard

The gold dollar is the standard unit of value of the United States and the secretary of the treasury is required to maintain at parity with the gold dollar all forms of money issued or coined by the United States. The government, however, does not permit the hoarding of gold, and issues gold certificates only to Federal Reserve banks. The present monetary system of the United States is, at least in these respects, different from the gold-standard system in operation prior to April, 1933. The present system is best described as a gold-bullion standard or a modified gold-standard system.

Silver now constitutes one-fourth of the monetary value in the proportion of silver to gold.

ONE DOLLAR (LIBERTY HEAD), 1849-1854

Specifics

U.S. Coin No: 86
Type: I Gold Dollar
Size: 8 or ½″
Weight: 25.8 grains
Edge: Reeded

Standard fineness: 900/1000
Quantity minted: 12,649,126
Proofs minted: None of record
Mint marks: c, d, o, and s
Designer: James Longacre

Description

Obverse: The gold dollar was authorized by the Act of March 3, 1849. Longacre used his daughter Sarah as his model. Liberty, facing left, wears a beaded-edge coronet inscribed with the word LIBERTY and placed well above the hair line. Shoulder-length tresses scroll to just below the truncation of the neck.

Thirteen six-point stars are equally indexed around the device and no further markings appear on the obverse field.

Reverse: Two half-wreaths of laurel, crossed at the stems and bound by a ribbon and single bow, form a wreath around the denomination, expressed with a large numeral "1" interposing the wreath ends. DOLLAR and the date are in two lines within the wreath. The issuing authority, UNITED STATES OF AMERICA, occupies the area around the device.

ONE DOLLAR (INDIAN HEAD/FEMALE), 1854-1856

Specifics

U.S. Coin No: 87
Type: II Gold Dollar
Size: 9 or 9/16″
Weight: 25.8 grains
Edge: Reeded

Standard fineness: 900/1000
Quantity minted: 849,487
Proofs minted: None of record
Mint marks: c, d, o, and s
Designer: James Longacre

Description

Obverse: A negative reaction to the size of the Type I gold dollar resulted in a slightly larger piece, Type II. James Longacre's model was the same as for the previous coin. This time, however, her headdress was changed to represent that of an American Indian princess.

The profile is smaller in area to allow for the extended height of the top feather of the seven that are arranged in the configuration of a crown. The headband, inscribed with LIBERTY, is separated from the plumes by a double row of beads. Liberty's hairdo is contained by the headdress and lengthy tresses involve the neck below the truncation.

The issuing authority, UNITED STATES OF AMERICA, surrounds the device.

Reverse: The denomination, expressed with a large numeral "1" and DOLLAR, is enclosed over the date in an agricultural wreath of corn, cotton, wheat, and tobacco, an arrangement readily identified with the designer.

ONE DOLLAR (INDIAN HEAD/FEMALE), 1856-1889

Specifics

U.S. Coin No: 88
Type: III Gold Dollar
Size: 9 or ⁹⁄₁₆″
Weight: 25.8
Edge: Reeded

Standard fineness: 900/1000
Quantity minted: 5,300,634
Proofs minted: 8,429 approx.
Mint marks: c, d, and s
Designer: James Longacre

Description

Obverse: The device on Type II, considered too small in proportion to the overall size of the coin, was redesigned by Longacre's use of a similar but noticeably different headdress. The configuration formed by the seven feathers is more confined than in the previous type, yet slightly extended. The headband, inscribed with LIBERTY, is separated from the plume arrangement by a single row of beads.

Liberty's hairdo is contained by the headdress and her tresses involve the neck and scroll under the truncation. The inscription UNITED STATES OF AMERICA is letterspaced in a smaller type face and encircles the device.

Reverse: The same agricultural wreath used on Type II dominates the field enclosing the denomination, expressed with a large numeral "1" and the word DOLLAR over the date.

QUARTER EAGLE ($2.50) (LIBERTY CAP/WITHOUT STARS), 1796

Specifics

U.S. Coin No: 89
Type: I Quarter Eagle
Size: 13 or $^{13}/_{16}''$
Weight: 67.5 grains
Edge: Reeded

Standard fineness: 916⅔/1000
Quantity minted: 897 approx.
Proofs minted: None of record
Mint marks: None
Designer: Robert Scot

Description

Obverse: The Quarter Eagle was authorized to be minted by the Act of April 2, 1792. Liberty, facing right, wears a Phrygian cap of a type rarely used as a symbol on United States coins. It rises much the same as a fez, while typical Phrygian caps lie flat or in folds. Her unkempt hair falls in all directions at the drape and is contained on the top by a veil that scrolls around the cap and into the hair.

The word LIBERTY is in the legend, and the date is radius in the base. No further markings appear on the field.

Reverse: A heraldic eagle displayed with a shield of the Union on his breast holds a bundle of arrows in his right talon and an olive branch in his left. The vertical pales or stripes in the shield are incorrectly arranged at eight white and seven red. No denomination is indicated.

Above the eagle, sixteen stars are embayed by six cloud puffs and a scroll in his beak is inscribed with the motto E PLURIBUS UNUM; UNITED STATES OF AMERICA circumvents the entire device. The border is denticled.

QUARTER EAGLE ($2.50), (LIBERTY CAP/WITH STARS), 1796-1807

Specifics

U.S. Coin No: 90
Type: II Quarter Eagle
Size: 13 or $13/16''$
Weight: 67.5 grains
Edge: Reeded

Standard fineness: 916⅔/1000
Quantity minted: 18,584
Proofs minted: None of record
Mint marks: None
Designer: Robert Scot

Description

Obverse: This type shows no appreciable difference over the previous Type I except for the addition of sixteen six-point stars flanking the device, eight on the left and eight on the right.

Reverse: The heraldic eagle displayed is identical to that used on Type I. The Union shield on his breast, with eight white stripes, or pales, and seven red, is larger than normal for a device of this kind. This is contrary to Great Seal specifications governing the stripes in the shield. Varieties of this type show thirteen stars on the obverse, eight left and five right, and thirteen and fourteen on the reverse. The border is denticled. Specimens prior to 1834 are rare.

QUARTER EAGLE ($2.50) (LIBERTY CAP), 1808

Specifics

U.S. Coin No: 91
Type: III Quarter Eagle
Size: 13 or 13⁄16″
Weight: 67.5 grains
Edge: Reeded

Standard fineness: 916⅔/1000
Quantity minted: 2,710
Proofs minted: None of record
Mint marks: None
Designer: John Reich

Description

Obverse: A matronly Liberty facing left, wears an unusually full cap that falls to the back instead of folding forward. The headband is inscribed with the word LIBERTY. Small tufts of hair protrude from the leading edge of the cap and back to a fall extending to a point below shoulder length to a scroll under the fold of the drape. The drape ties are gathered and pinned just under a curl on the neck. Thirteen stars flank the device —seven on the left and six on the right. The date is radius in the base.

Reverse: An eagle displayed with an olive branch in his right talon and three broad-head arrows in his left and a Union shield on his breast. A scroll in radius from one wing to the other is inscribed E PLURIBUS UNUM. The denomination is expressed by the numeral "2½" and the letter D. The inscription UNITED STATES OF AMERICA completely involves the device.

QUARTER EAGLE ($2.50) (LIBERTY CAP), 1821-1834

Specifics

U.S. Coin No: 92
Type: IV Quarter Eagle
Size: 12 or ¾″
Weight: 67.5 grains
Edge: Reeded

Standard fineness: 916⅔/1000
Quantity minted: 42,065
Proofs minted: None of record
Mint marks: None
Designer: Robert Scot

Description

Obverse: There were no Quarter Eagles minted between 1808 and 1821. When coining was resumed, Liberty's likeness, still facing left, was altered slightly. The fullness of the cap was restored to its normal size and the head was reduced in accordance with the overall diameter of the coin. Liberty's neck appeared considerably shorter and heavier due to omission of the drape. Thirteen stars indexed the area next to the border and the date was in radius in the base.

Reverse: The motif is very similar to the preceding Type III. The motto E PLURIBUS UNUM is in the scroll above the eagle; the figure "2½" and the letter D designate the denomination below; and the issuing authority parallels the denticled border from the olive branch to the arrows.

The size was reduced in 1829 to 11 or ¹¹⁄₁₆″.

QUARTER EAGLE ($2.50) (CLASSIC HEAD), 1834-1839

Specifics

U.S. Coin No: 93

Type: V Quarter Eagle

Size: 11 or $1\frac{1}{16}''$

Weight: 64.5 grains

Edge: Reeded

Standard fineness: 899.225/1000

900/1000 in 1837

Quantity minted: 968,289

Proofs minted: None of record

Mint marks: C, D, and O

Designer: William Kneass

Description

The Act of June 28, 1834, authorized a reduction in the weight, size, and fineness of the Quarter Eagle. In 1837 the fineness was increased by the Act of January 18th.

Obverse: This design by Kneass shows Liberty facing left with a wavy hairdo contained by a headband inscribed LIBERTY. Her tresses fall in a small and large scroll to the base of the neck with the larger scroll extending below the truncation.

Thirteen stars index the inside border and the date is in radius in the base. The border pattern is denticled.

Reverse: An eagle supports a Union shield disproportionate with the device. In his left talon are three broad-head arrows, and in his right, an olive branch. The denomination is indicated by the numeral "2½" and the letter D, and UNITED STATES OF AMERICA surrounds the device.

QUARTER EAGLE ($2.50) (CORONET), 1840-1907

Specifics

U.S. Coin No: 94
Type: VI Quarter Eagle
Size: 11 or $11/16''$
Weight: 64.5 grains
Edge: Reeded

Standard fineness: 900/1000
Quantity minted: 12,200,225
Proofs minted: 4,047
Mint marks: C, D, S, and O
Designer: Christian Gobrecht

Description

Obverse: The Gobrecht obverse was not transposed as faithfully on this coin as it was on the Half Eagle and Eagle. Liberty faces left with her hair contained in a bun and ornamented with a strand of beads. A coronet bearing the word LIBERTY tops the forepart of the head and the hair at the back, and two tresses scroll down toward the pedestal of the device—one at the extreme back and one centered above the shoulder line.

Thirteen stars encompass the device and the date is in the base.

Reverse: The eagle displayed here is not too unlike the preceding type, except that he is positioned higher in the field and shows a smaller shield on his breast. Three broad-head arrows are grasped by the left talon, and an olive branch pointing upward is held in the right talon.

The denomination is indicated as 2½ D. with the issuing authority, UNITED STATES OF AMERICA, embracing the whole of the device.

211

QUARTER EAGLE ($2.50) (INDIAN HEAD/MALE), 1908-1929

Specifics

U.S. Coin No: 95

Type: VII Quarter Eagle

Size: 11 or 11⁄16″

Weight: 64.5 grains

Edge: Reeded

Standard fineness: 900/1000

Quantity minted: 7,252,088

Proofs minted: 1,728

Mint marks: D only

Designer: Bela Lyon Pratt

Description

Obverse: This completely new approach to design and coinage was the first intaglio impression produced for general circulation by the mint. Intaglio is, in a sense, the opposite of cameo: The design is in relief but literally "pushed" below the surface, with the highest point in the relief barely equal to the plane of the coin. There is no border pattern.

The Indian Head (male), facing left, is attired in the most realistic of headdresses in comparison to other Indian Head designs. The word LIBERTY is curved on the periphery above, and the date below. Six five-point stars edge the left side of the field, and seven the right side.

Reverse: A stately eagle, perched on a bundle of arrows and superimposed by a scrolled olive branch, is flanked on the left by E PLURIBUS UNUM in three lines, and on the right, by IN GOD WE TRUST in four lines. UNITED STATES OF AMERICA is in the legend and 2½ DOLLARS in the base. The designer's initials, BLP, appear over the date.

THREE DOLLARS (INDIAN HEAD/FEMALE), 1854-1889

Specifics

U.S. Coin No: 96
Type: I Three Dollars, Gold
Size: 13 or 13⁄16″
Weight: 77.4 grains
Edge: Reeded

Standard fineness: 900/1000
Quantity minted: 539,883
Proofs minted: 1,949
Mint marks: s, D, and o
Designer: James Longacre

Description

The Three-Dollar Gold Piece was not anticipated in the original Act of April 2, 1792, and when the government reduced postage rates from five cents to three cents, it was felt that the Three-Dollar coin would influence and facilitate three-cent postage transaction. It was finally authorized by the Act of February 21, 1853.

Obverse: The device is identical to that of another designed by Longacre, the One-Dollar coin. The headband bearing the word LIBERTY is beaded on both edges and the plume arrangement is the same as on the earlier coin. Proportionately, the device is larger and the inscription, UNITED STATES OF AMERICA, is not letterspaced.

Reverse: An agricultural wreath identical to the one on the Gold Dollar encloses the denomination, expressed below the date with a large numeral "3" subordinated by the word DOLLARS. The border is denticled.

HALF EAGLE ($5.00) (LIBERTY CAP/SMALL EAGLE), 1795-1796

Specifics

U.S. Coin No: 97
Type: I Half Eagle, Gold
Size: 16 or 1″
Weight: 135 grains
Edge: Reeded

Standard fineness: 916⅔/1000
Quantity minted: Inaccurate record
Proofs minted: None of record
Mint marks: None
Designer: Robert Scot

Description

This is the first gold coin struck under the authority of the Coinage Act of April 2, 1792. The device is almost identical to that of the Quarter Eagle, except for details in the veil wrapped around the base of the cap.

Obverse: Fifteen stars flank the profile of Liberty—ten on the left and five on the right. This is one star short of the Quarter-Eagle count. The word LIBERTY in the legend arches the forehead and face—another difference in the two coins. The date, in the base, is similar.

Reverse: On an attractive departure from the usual design, a fledgling eagle with raised wings grips in his talons a palm branch and with his beak holds upright a laurel wreath.

There is no indication of the denomination on this coin. The issuing authority, UNITED STATES OF AMERICA, parallels the border with the UNI and the last A in AMERICA touching the leaves of the palm branch.

HALF EAGLE ($5.00) (LIBERTY CAP/HERALDIC EAGLE), 1795-1807

Specifics

U.S. Coin No: 98
Type: II Half Eagle, Gold
Size: 16 or 1"
Weight: 135 grains
Edge: Reeded

Standard fineness: 916⅔/1000
Quantity minted: Inaccurate record
Proofs minted: None of record
Mint marks: None
Designer: Robert Scot

Description

Obverse: Type II is almost identical to Type I except for the star arrangement and count. Some show fifteen stars with ten on the left and five on the right; others, sixteen stars with eleven on the left and five on the right; while a third variety has eight left and five right.

Reverse: The heraldic-eagle design has an eagle displayed with a Union shield showing seven red stripes and eight white. One variety of shield correctly contains six red and seven white, and another, thirteen stars embayed above the eagle. A third type has fourteen stars.

There are thirteen arrows in the eagle's right talon and an olive branch in his left. A scroll in his beak is inscribed E PLURIBUS UNUM, and surrounding the entire device is an inscription of the issuing authority, UNITED STATES OF AMERICA.

HALF EAGLE ($5.00) (LIBERTY CAP), 1807-1812

Specifics

U.S. Coin No: 99
Type: III Half Eagle
Size: 16 or 1"
Weight: 135 grains
Edge: Reeded

Standard fineness: 916⅔/1000
Quantity minted: 1,784,625
Proofs minted: None of record
Mint marks: None
Designer: John Reich

Description

Obverse: Reich's full slave's cap makes this type noticeably different from the others with a soft cap. Liberty faces left, with small tufts of hair protruding from under the lead edge of the headband inscribed LIBERTY. Her extremely long tresses turn down and beyond the shoulder line and end in a forward scroll under the drape fold.

Seven stars parallel the left border and six the right. The letterspaced date is in radius in the base.

Reverse: A short-winged eagle holds a large olive branch in his right talon and three broad-head arrows in his left. A Union shield is on his breast, and the motto E PLURIBUS UNUM is inscribed on a scroll arched above his head.

For the first time in this series the denomination is expressed on the coin: It appears under the eagle as the numeral "5" and the letter D. The inscription, UNITED STATES OF AMERICA, encircles the entire device.

HALF EAGLE ($5.00) (LIBERTY CAP), 1813-1834

Specifics

U.S. Coin No: 100

Type: IV Half Eagle

Size: 16 or 1″

Weight: 135 grains

Edge: Reeded

Standard fineness: 916⅔/1000

Quantity minted: 1,385,612

Proofs minted: None of record

Mint marks: None

Designer: Robert Scot

Description

Obverse: Scot changed the Reich obverse by creating a larger head and reducing the fullness of the cap. His Liberty, facing left, seems to have more-than-sufficient hair, confined nevertheless to the new truncation, which shows no shoulder line.

Thirteen six-point stars index the device, and the date is in the base.

Reverse: The eagle is similar in many ways to that of the preceding type except for his oversized head and neck. An olive branch in his right talon is different and the arrows, with larger broadheads, are spread farther apart.

The motto E PLURIBUS UNUM on the scroll and the surrounding issuing authority, UNITED STATES OF AMERICA, remain essentially the same, along with the manner in which the denomination is indicated, with a numeral "5" and the letter D. Large denticles make up the border pattern.

The Half Eagles dated 1829 and later are smaller in diameter.

HALF EAGLE ($5.00) (CLASSIC HEAD), 1834-1838

Specifics

U.S. Coin No: 101
Type: V Half Eagle
Size: 14 or ⅞″
Weight: 129 grains
Edge: Reeded

Standard fineness: 899.225/1000
      900/1000 in 1837
Quantity minted: 2,114,180
Proofs minted: None of record
Mint marks: c and d
Designer: William Kneass

Description

Obverse: The weight, fineness, and size of the Half Eagle were authorized reduced by the Act of June 28, 1834. The fineness was then ordered increased by the Act of January 18, 1837.

In his new conception, Kneass abandoned the slave's cap in favor of the fillet-type headband inscribed LIBERTY. Liberty herself is much thinner through the neck, with her tresses exceeding shoulder length and scrolled back to the truncation.

Thirteen stars form an area pattern inside the border and the date is slightly in radius in the base.

Reverse: A noticeably disproportionate eagle occupies the center of the field with a shield of the Union on his breast, an oversize branch of olive in his right talon and three broad-head arrows in his left. The denomination 5D. is below the eagle and the issuing authority around him.

HALF EAGLE ($5.00) (CORONET/WITHOUT MOTTO), 1839-1866

Specifics

U.S. Coin No: 102
Type: VI Half Eagle
Size: 14 or ⅞″
Weight: 129 grains
Edge: Reeded

Standard fineness: 900/1000
Quantity minted: 8,694,434
Proofs minted: 268
Mint marks: c, d, o, and s
Designer: Christian Gobrecht

Description

Obverse: Unlike the Quarter Eagle of the Coronet type, the head of Liberty on this coin is a credit to Gobrecht's artistic talents. It has a definite Roman configuration to the profile, with a strand of hair scrolling down the center line of the neck and another at the back of the neck. Liberty faces left with her hair well-contained in a bun at the back and decorated with a strand of beads. Thirteen stars encircle the device, with a radius date in the base.

Reverse: The eagle, with a smaller shield on his breast, has returned to a much more realistic proportion. He holds three arrows in his left talon and a livelier olive branch in his right.

The motto has been omitted but the issuing authority, UNITED STATES OF AMERICA, and the expression for the denomination, FIVE D., encompass the entire device.

HALF EAGLE ($5.00) (CORONET/WITH MOTTO), 1866-1908

Specifics

U.S. Coin No: 103
Type: VII Half Eagle
Size: 14 or 7/8"
Weight: 129 grains
Edge: Reeded

Standard fineness: 900/1000
Quantity minted: 47,181,832
Proofs minted: 2,927
Mint marks: CC, O, D, and S
Designer: Christian Gobrecht

Description

Obverse: There is no appreciable difference between this obverse design by Gobrecht and that of the previous type. Liberty, facing left, wears a coronet and her hair is confined in a bun with a strand of beads.

Reverse: The eagle remains unaltered but the inscription UNITED STATES OF AMERICA is shown in larger type face, which gives the design added strength.

The motto IN GOD WE TRUST has been inscribed on a scroll above the eagle's head.

Both sides have denticled border patterns.

HALF EAGLE ($5.00) (INDIAN HEAD/MALE), 1908-1929

Specifics

U.S. Coin No: 104
Type: VIII Half Eagle
Size: 14 or ⅛″
Weight: 129 grains
Edge: Reeded

Standard fineness: 900/1000
Quantity minted: 14,079,242
Proofs minted: 1,077
Mint marks: D, O, and S
Designer: Bela Lyon Pratt

Description

Obverse: The Type VIII is a companion piece to the Type VII Quarter Eagle. Intaglio engraving gives the effect of relief although the design actually lies below the general surface of the coin. When this coin was proposed, it brought negative comments from all quarters of the government, its critics claiming the recesses would provide space for dirt and contamination. Others more correctly called attention to the inherent difficulties that would be encountered in stacking.

The Indian head (male), facing left, wears an accurately detailed headdress. The word LIBERTY and the date curve on the periphery along with six five-point stars on the left and seven on the right. BLP, the designer's initials, are above the date.

Reverse: An eagle perched on a bundle of arrows superimposed by a curved bow of olive is flanked left by the motto E PLURIBUS UNUM, and right, by the motto IN GOD WE TRUST; UNITED STATES OF AMERICA and the denomination FIVE DOLLARS are at top and bottom.

EAGLE ($10.00) (LIBERTY CAP/SMALL EAGLE), 1795-1797

Specifics

U.S. Coin No: 105
Type: I Eagle
Size: 21 of 1⁵⁄₁₆″
Weight: 270 grains
Edge: Reeded

Standard fineness: 916⅔/1000
Quantity minted: 12,195
Proofs minted: None of record
Mint marks: None
Designer: Robert Scot

Description

Obverse: Authorization for the Eagle was provided in the Coinage Act of April 2, 1792. Scot's concept of Liberty, facing right, wears an unusual form of the Phrygian slave's cap. It is peaked and best described as representing a fez. Mr. Scot used the same style of pileus on the Half and Quarter Eagles. The veil holding the cap in place scrolls into the hairdo, allowing a small tuft to protrude from the lead edge and the longer tresses to turn downward in an unruly manner.

Sixteen stars line the inner border—eight to a side—with LIBERTY in the legend and the date in radius in the base.

Reverse: A fledgling eagle is displayed, gripping a palm branch in his talons and holding ·a laurel wreath upright with his beak. There is no indication of the denomination on this coin, but the issuing authority, UNITED STATES OF AMERICA, almost surrounds the reverse device.

EAGLE ($10.00) (LIBERTY CAP/HERALDIC EAGLE), 1797-1804

Specifics

U.S. Coin No: 106
Type: II Eagle
Size: 21 or 1⁵⁄₁₆"
Weight: 270 grains
Edge: Reeded

Standard fineness: 916⅔/1000
Quantity minted: 108,308
Proofs minted: None of record
Mint marks: None
Designer: Robert Scot

Description

Obverse: Scot changed the design on this type in its organization only, enlarging the main device slightly. One variety has a sixteen-star border arrangement with ten on the left and six on the right. Another has a total of thirteen with nine on the left and four on the right. A third and fourth varieties have seven stars on the left and six on the right, and eight on the left with five on the right respectively. This is important because it changes the position of the word LIBERTY—which enters into the authentication of a high-value coin.

Reverse: The heraldic eagle has a Union shield on his breast with an incorrect arrangement of seven red and six white stripes. In his right talon he holds thirteen arrows, and in his left, an olive branch. Six cloud puffs embay thirteen stars above the eagle's head; inscribed in a scroll in his beak is the motto E PLURIBUS UNUM, and around the device, UNITED STATES OF AMERICA.

EAGLE ($10.00) (CORONET/WITHOUT MOTTO), 1838-1866

Specifics

U.S. Coin No: 107
Type: III Eagle
Size: 17 or 1¹⁄₁₆″
Weight: 258 grains
Edge: Reeded

Standard fineness: 900/1000
Quantity minted: 5,304,338
Proofs minted: 259—incomplete
Mint marks: o and s
Designer: Christian Gobrecht

Description

Obverse: The weight, size, and fineness of the Eagle were reduced by authority of the Act of June 28, 1834. An Act of January 18, 1837, increased the fineness.

Gobrecht's Liberty, facing left, wears a coronet inscribed with the word LIBERTY. Her hair is neatly confined in a double bun on the back of her head by a strand of beads. A crescent tuft sweeps to a point back over the ear and two tresses scroll toward the pedestal of the neck—one on the side and one to the back. Thirteen stars index the area within the border, and the date is in the base.

Reverse: A short-winged eagle bearing a Union shield on his breast holds an olive branch in his right talon and three arrows in his left. The denomination is expressed as TEN D. at the bottom, and UNITED STATES OF AMERICA is inscribed around the device.

EAGLE ($10.00) (CORONET/WITH MOTTO), 1866-1907

Specifics

U.S. Coin No: 108
Type: IV Eagle
Size: 17 or 1⅟₁₆″
Weight: 258 grains
Edge: Reeded

Standard fineness: 900/1000
Quantity minted: 36,382,594
Proofs minted: 2,293
Mint marks: s, cc, o, and d
Designer: Christian Gobrecht

Description

Obverse: Liberty, facing left, wears a coronet bearing the word LIBERTY. Her hair is contained at the back in two buns secured by a string of beads. Two strands of hair scroll down the neck—one on a center line with the pedestal and the second at the back.

An unusual radius in the pedestal gives the device a pleasing finish over the normal truncation. The date lies in a slight reverse in radius with the base. Thirteen stars envolve the head from right to left of the date.

Reverse: Neither the eagle nor his position has changed. His feathers are not so coarsely defined, but general configuration lines are basically the same as in the preceding device. He is holding an olive branch and three arrows in his right and left talons, while below him in the base is the denomination, TEN D. The inscription UNITED STATES OF AMERICA runs around the balance of the design and the motto IN GOD WE TRUST is visible on a scroll above the eagle's head.

EAGLE ($10.00) (INDIAN HEAD/WITHOUT MOTTO), 1907-1908

Specifics

U.S. Coin No: 109	*Standard fineness:* 900/1000
Type: V Eagle	*Quantity minted:* 483,448
Size: 17 or 1⅟₁₆″	*Proofs minted:* None of record
Weight: 258 grains	*Mint marks:* D only
Edge: Starred—46 count	*Designer:* Augustus Saint-Gaudens

Description

Obverse: This is the fourth in a series of Indian headdresses to become a part of United States coinage art. It was introduced into our system by Saint-Gaudens, considered by many of the severest critics the finest of modern sculptors.

In her new role, Liberty faces left. The contour of her headdress conforms to the contour of the inner rim, separated by thirteen stars, five of which lie forward of the first feather. LIBERTY is inscribed on the band of the feathered bonnet and the date—rather large—is in the base. There are forty-six stars on the edge in place of reedings.

Reverse: An eagle perched, not unlike the eagle on the Pratt Five-Dollar Gold Piece. He is standing on a bundle of arrows graced by an olive branch, below which is the denomination, TEN DOLLARS. The issuing authority is in the legend, and at the eagle's back, the motto E PLURIBUS UNUM appears in three lines. The border is plain.

EAGLE ($10.00) (INDIAN HEAD/WITH MOTTO), 1908-1933

Specifics

U.S. Coin No: 110

Type: VI Eagle

Size: 17 or 1¹⁄₁₆″

Weight: 258 grains

Edge: Starred—46 count to 1912;
48 count after 1912

Standard fineness: 900/1000

Quantity minted: 14,385,907

Proofs minted: 768

Mint marks: D and S

Designer: Augustus Saint-Gaudens

Description

President Theodore Roosevelt tried desperately to keep the motto IN GOD WE TRUST from becoming a part of any United States coin. For awhile he succeeded, but in the case of this gold piece, Congress over-ruled him and it was placed on the reverse field in the second year of its minting.

Note the resemblance between the Bela Lyon Pratt Five-Dollar reverse and the Augustus Saint-Gaudens reverse.

227

DOUBLE EAGLE ($20.00) (CORONET/WITHOUT MOTTO), 1849-1866

Specifics

U.S. Coin No: 111
Type: I Double Eagle
Size: 21 or 1⅝₁₆″
Weight: 516 grains
Edge: Reeded

Standard fineness: 900/1000
Quantity minted: 23,514,279
Proofs minted: 140—incomplete
Mint marks: o and s
Designer: James Longacre

Description

Obverse: This, the greatest of American gold coins both in size and value, was also designed by Longacre. Naturally he used his daughter's original poses for the obverse. The Double Eagle was authorized minted by the Act of March 3, 1849. There were no increases or reductions in its weight or fineness until it was discontinued under the Gold Reserve Act of January 30, 1934.

Liberty, wearing a coronet, faces left. The beaded-edge headpiece is inscribed LIBERTY and rests well back from the forward hair line, allowing the hair to rise over the edge and down in a scroll to the pedestal. Thirteen stars and the date encircle the device.

Reverse: What appears to be the outline of an ornate shield is actually an elaborate scroll bearing the motto E PLURIBUS UNUM, behind which stands an eagle, a shield on his breast and arrows and an olive branch in his talons. An oval of thirteen stars lies within a rayed glory above his head. The issuing authority, UNITED STATES OF AMERICA, and the denomination TWENTY-D encompass the device.

DOUBLE EAGLE ($20.00) (CORONET/WITH MOTTO), 1866-1876

Specifics

U.S. Coin No: 112
Type: II Double Eagle
Size: 21 or 1⁵⁄₁₆″
Weight: 516 grains
Edge: Reeded

Standard fineness: 900/1000
Quantity minted: 16,161,143
Proofs minted: 335
Mint marks: cc and s
Designer: James Longacre

Description

The obverse of Longacre's Double Eagle did not change with this type. The postwar period was causing some concern among the general public in the area of religion, and Congress, in turn, pressured the treasury to incorporate the motto IN GOD WE TRUST on all coinage.

The illustration at the right shows how this motto was adapted to the reverse design.

DOUBLE EAGLE ($20.00) (CORONET), 1877-1907

Specifics

U.S. Coin No: 113
Type: III Double Eagle
Size: 21 or 1⁵⁄₁₆″
Weight: 516 grains
Edge: Reeded

Standard fineness: 900/1000
Quantity minted: 64,429,851
Proofs minted: 2,311
Mint marks: CC, S, O, and D
Designer: James Longacre

Description

A second and third change in the reverse are barely noticeable unless called to the viewer's attention. The shield on Type II was upgraded from the squared sides on Type I to the scrolled sides shown below.

On closer examination, major differences between the ornamental scrolls can be seen on all three types.

The qualifying feature that distinguishes this Type III by Longacre is the conversion of the denomination to a full reading of TWENTY DOLLARS.

The border pattern is denticled.

DOUBLE EAGLE ($20.00) (STANDING LIBERTY— ROMAN NUMERALS), 1907

Specifics

U.S. Coin No: 114
Type: IV Double Eagle
Size: 21 or 1⅜₁₆″
Weight: 516 grains
Edge: Stars and letters

Standard fineness: 900/1000
Quantity minted: 11,250
Proofs minted: Not recorded
Mint marks: None
Designer: Augustus Saint-Gaudens

Description

Obverse: Saint-Gaudens' Liberty, standing on a plane with her left foot on a higher level, is draped in a loose, flowing garment drawn up at the shoulders, leaving the arms bare and the forepart of her feet exposed. Her hair is almost waist length and flows to the left in back of a torch held in her right hand. In her left hand, which is extended toward the border, she holds an olive branch that interposes four of the forty-six five-point stars that constitute the border. The Capitol's dome can be detected at about seven o'clock between the lower folds of Liberty's drape and the border. The monotony of the plain field is broken by a series of the sun's rays. LIBERTY appears in the legend, and the date, MCMVII, in Roman numerals is to the right of the figure's left leg, between the second and third star from the end.

Reverse: An eagle in free flight to the left with the issuing authority, UNITED STATES OF AMERICA, and the denomination, TWENTY DOLLARS.

DOUBLE EAGLE ($20.00) (STANDING LIBERTY/ ARABIC NUMERALS), 1907-1908

Specifics

U.S. Coin No: 115

Type: V Double Eagle

Size: 21 or 1⁵⁄₁₆″

Weight: 516 grains

Edge: Starred and lettered

Standard fineness: 900/1000

Quantity minted: 5,296,968

Proofs minted: None

Mint marks: D only

Designer: Augustus Saint-Gaudens

Description

The second issue of Saint-Gaudens' Double Eagle was provided with a rim that did not exist on Type IV. The lettered edge reads E PLURIBUS UNUM, intermittent with stars.

Close examination of the Capitol Building in the extreme lower left border area on Type IV and this coin shows a difference in concept. The eagle on this piece is also more detailed than its predecessor.

The illustrations at the right compare the Roman numerals of Type IV's date with the Arabic date of Type V.

DOUBLE EAGLE ($20.00) (STANDING LIBERTY/ WITH MOTTO), 1908-1933

Specifics

U.S. Coin No: 116
Type: VI Double Eagle
Size: 21 or 1⁵⁄₁₆″
Weight: 516 grains
Edge: Starred and lettered

Standard fineness: 900/1000
Quantity minted: 64,536,365
Proofs minted: 687
Mint marks: D and S
Designer: Augustus Saint-Gaudens

Description

Both the obverse and reverse on the regular issue coinage have assumed the properties of a rimmed coin other than the date. The motto IN GOD WE TRUST is all that has been added to this, our largest and last gold coin.

The illustrations at the right show in detail the motto and its location.

Double eagles dated 1907 to 1912 displayed 46 stars in their border patterns. This number was increased to 48 on issues from 1912 to 1933.

CHAPTER VIII

THE CONDITION
AND GRADING OF COINS

A coin of the United States can have as many as four values, all legitimate and each worthy of consideration in any appraisal concerning a high-value coin. Two of these values are affected by the condition of the coin, and two are not.

The first, its denomination or fixed value, is minimal since no U.S. coin, current or not, ever depreciates in value. The second value, its "price," which is usually less than the established value, depends on what a dealer is willing to give or accept in exchange for the coin. "Price" range may vary with the condition of a coin.

The third "value" is that determined by demand and is the estimated equivalent available on the open market—not through a dealer's market. It never implies a coin is for sale and here again condition dictates the terms.

Fourth is its "esteemed" value, which is rarely quoted in dollars and cents. This figure may be affected by a coin's rarity or the sentimental attachment of the owner, which makes the coin invaluable to him. His esteem for it may render it "priceless." Coins have been known to sell at the esteemed value.

The following illustrations show three of the six grading classifications most often encountered in circulated coins: good, fine, and extremely fine.*

---

* The six principal grading categories recognized by the numismatic industry are available in *A Guide to the Grading of United States Coins,* by M. R. Brown and J. W. Dunn, Racine, Wisconsin, Whitman Publishing Company, 1969. It is recommended for more accurate grading from poor to uncirculated conditions.

NICKEL FIVE-CENT PIECES

Without CENTS 1883

	Quan. Minted	Good	V.G.	Fine	E.F.	Unc.	Proof
1883 Without CENTS							
....(5,219)	5,479,519	$1.10	$1.50	$2.25	$4.00	$9.00	$48.00

With CENTS 1883-1913   Location of mint mark

		Good	V.G.	Fine	E.F.	Unc.	Proof
1883 With CENTS							
....(6,783)	16,032,983	4.50	6.00	8.50	15.00	40.00	62.50
1884.....(3,942)	11,273,942	4.50	6.25	10.00	17.50	42.50	62.50
1885.....(3,790)	1,476,490	55.00	70.00	95.00	150.00	250.00	340.00
1886.....(4,290)	3,330,290	27.50	37.50	50.00	75.00	125.00	175.00
1887.....(2,960)	15,263,652	2.75	3.75	6.00	12.00	35.00	55.00
1888.....(4,582)	10,720,483	4.50	7.25	11.00	20.00	35.00	60.00
1889.....(3,336)	15,881,361	2.75	3.75	5.50	11.00	35.00	50.00
1890.....(2,740)	16,259,272	3.75	4.75	7.00	15.00	35.00	50.00
1891.....(2,350)	16,834,350	2.75	3.75	6.00	11.00	35.00	50.00
1892.....(2,745)	11,699,642	3.00	4.00	6.25	12.00	35.00	57.50
1893.....(2,195)	13,370,195	2.50	3.75	5.50	11.00	35.00	57.50
1894.....(2,632)	5,413,132	4.50	6.50	10.00	16.50	47.50	70.00
1895.....(2,062)	9,979,884	1.75	3.00	5.25	10.00	37.50	62.50
1896.....(1,862)	8,842,920	2.25	4.25	8.50	18.50	50.00	115.00
1897.....(1,938)	20,428,735	1.25	2.00	3.50	8.00	30.00	57.50
1898.....(1,795)	12,532,087	1.25	2.00	3.50	8.00	30.00	57.50
1899.....(2,031)	26,029,031	1.00	1.50	2.75	7.25	30.00	55.00
1900.....(2,262)	27,255,995	.60	1.25	2.25	5.75	26.00	55.00
1901.....(1,985)	26,480,213	.50	1.00	2.00	5.00	25.00	55.00
1902.....(2,018)	31,489,579	.50	1.00	2.00	5.00	25.00	55.00
1903.....(1,790)	28,006,725	.50	1.00	2.00	5.00	25.00	55.00
1904.....(1,817)	21,404,984	.50	1.00	2.00	5.00	25.00	55.00
1905.....(2,152)	29,827,276	.50	1.00	2.00	5.00	25.00	55.00
1906.....(1,725)	38,613,725	.50	1.00	2.00	5.00	25.00	55.00
1907.....(1,475)	39,214,800	.50	1.00	2.00	5.00	25.00	75.00
1908.....(1,620)	22,686,177	.50	1.00	2.00	5.00	25.00	55.00
1909.....(4,763)	11,590,526	.75	1.25	2.50	6.00	27.50	52.50
1910.....(2,405)	30,169,353	.50	1.00	2.00	5.00	25.00	55.00
1911.....(1,733)	39,559,372	.50	1.00	2.00	5.00	25.00	55.00
1912.....(2,145)	26,236,714	.50	1.00	2.00	5.00	25.00	55.00
1912D............8,474,000		1.25	2.00	5.00	40.00	200.00	
1912S.............238,000		25.00	32.50	45.00	100.00	375.00	
1913 Liberty Hd. (5 Known)				A.N.A. Sale 1967 46,000			

[91]

Page 91 reproduced from the 25th edition of the famous Red Book, R. S. Yeoman's *A Guide Book of United States Coins*, illustrates the six (6) possible conditions that can affect the value of a coin. Use of the Red Book is recommended as a supporting reference for all coin evaluations.

HALF DOLLARS

Designer John Reich; weight 13.48 grams; composition: .8924 silver, .1076 copper; approx. diameter 32.5 mm; edge varieties, 1807-1814: FIFTY CENTS OR HALF A DOLLAR; 1814-1831: star added between DOLLAR and FIFTY; 1832-1836: vertical lines added between words.

First style 1807-1808

1807 Small Stars	1807 Large Stars	1807, 50 over 20			

	Quan. Minted	Good	V.G.	Fine	V.F.	E.F.	Unc.
1807 small stars....	} 750,500	$20.00	$27.50	$40.00	$85.00	$150.00	$450.00
1807 large stars.....		17.50	25.00	37.50	70.00	110.00	350.00
1807 same, 50 over 20.....		17.50	25.00	37.50	70.00	115.00	360.00
1808, 8 over 7....	} 1,368,600	12.50	19.00	30.00	42.50	65.00	180.00
1808............		10.00	12.50	17.50	27.50	45.00	140.00

Remodeled Portrait and Eagle 1809-1834

1809 experimental edge, xxxx between words

1809 experimental edge, ııııı between words

		Good	V.G.	Fine	V.F.	E.F.	Unc.
1809 normal......	} 1,405,810	10.00	12.50	16.00	26.00	40.00	130.00
1809 xxxx edge ..		13.00	20.00	32.50	45.00	67.50	175.00
1809 ıııııı edge...		12.50	19.00	30.00	42.50	65.00	160.00
1810............1,276,276		10.00	12.50	16.00	24.00	40.00	125.00

[128]

Page 128 from the Red Book demonstrates factors other than the surface condition of a coin that may also affect its value. For that reason any serious attempt to appraise or evaluate a coin should be in conjunction with the leading reference as an accepted standard in the industry—*A Guide Book of United States Coins.*

U.S. Coin No. 1

| Good | Fine | Ex-Fine |

U.S. Coin No. 2

| Good | Fine | Ex-Fine |

U.S. Coin No. 3

| Good | Fine | Ex-Fine |

U.S. Coin No. 4

| Good | Fine | Ex-Fine |

U.S. Coin No. 5

Good	Fine	Ex-Fine

U.S. Coin No. 6

Good	Fine	Ex-Fine

| Good | Fine | Ex-Fine |

| Good | Fine | Ex-Fine |

U.S. Coin No. 9

| Good | Fine | Ex-Fine |

U.S. Coin No. 10

| Good | Fine | Ex-Fine |

U.S. Coin No. 11

Good	Fine	Ex-Fine

U.S. Coin No. 12

Good	Fine	Ex-Fine

U.S. Coin No. 13

Good   Fine   Ex-Fine

U.S. Coin No. 14. Nos. 15 and 16 Obverse and Old Reverse

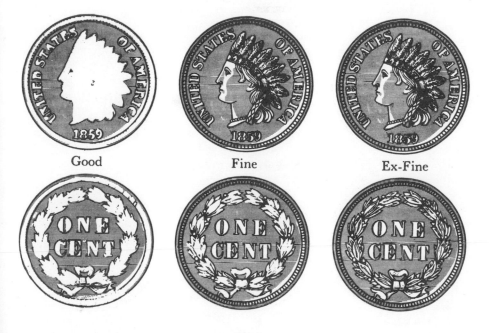

Good   Fine   Ex-Fine

U.S. Coin Nos. 15 and 16 New Reverse

U.S. Coin Nos. 17, 18, 19, and 20

Old Reverse Coins

New Reverse Coins

U.S. Coin No. 21

Good   Fine   Ex-Fine

U.S. Coin No. 22

Good   Fine   Ex-Fine

U.S. Coin No. 23

Good

Fine

Ex-Fine

U.S. Coin Nos. 24 and 25

Good

Fine

Ex-Fine

U.S. Coin Nos. 26 and 27

Good	Fine	Ex-Fine

U.S. Coin Nos. 28 and 29

Good	Fine	Ex-Fine

U.S. Coin Nos. 30 and 31

Good

Fine

Ex-Fine

U.S. Coin Nos. 32 and 33

Good

Fine

Ex-Fine

U.S. Coin No. 34

Good	Fine	Ex-Fine

U.S. Coin Nos. 35 and 41

Good	Fine	Ex-Fine

U.S. Coin Nos. 36 and 42

| Good | Fine | Ex-Fine |

U.S. Coin Nos. 37 and 43

| Good | Fine | Ex-Fine |

U.S. Coin Nos. 38 and 44

Good   Fine   Ex-Fine

U.S. Coin Nos. 39 and 45

Good   Fine   Ex-Fine

U.S. Coin Nos. 40 and 46

| Good | Fine | Ex-Fine |

U.S. Coin No. 47

| Good | Fine | Ex-Fine |

U.S. Coin No. 48

Good   Fine   Ex-Fine

U.S. Coin Nos. 49 and 50

Good   Fine   Ex-Fine

U.S. Coin No. 51

Good   Fine   Ex-Fine

U.S. Coin Nos. 52 and 65

Good   Fine   Ex-Fine

U.S. Coin Nos. 53 and 66

Good

Fine

Ex-Fine

U.S. Coin Nos. 54 and 67

Good

Fine

Ex-Fine

U.S. Coin Nos. 55, 68, and 69

Good	Fine	Ex-Fine

U.S. Coin Nos. 56, 70, and 81

Good	Fine	Ex-Fine

U.S. Coin Nos. 57 and 71

Good   Fine   Ex-Fine

U.S. Coin Nos. 58, 72, and 82

Good   Fine   Ex-Fine

U.S. Coin Nos. 59 and 73

Good	Fine	Ex-Fine

U.S. Coin Nos. 60 and 61

Good	Fine	Ex-Fine

U.S. Coin Nos. 62 and 63

Good   Fine   Ex-Fine

U.S. Coin Nos. 64 and 78

Good   Fine   Ex-Fine

U.S. Coin No. 74

| Good | Fine | Ex-Fine |

U.S. Coin No. 75

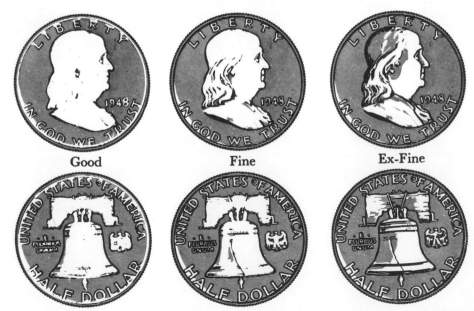

| Good | Fine | Ex-Fine |

U.S. Coin Nos. 76 and 77

| Good | Fine | Ex-Fine |

U.S. Coin No. 79

| Good | Fine | Ex-Fine |

U.S. Coin No. 80

Good	Fine	Ex-Fine

U.S. Coin No. 83 Trade Dollar

Good	Fine	Ex-Fine

U.S. Coin No. 84

Good   Fine   Ex-Fine

U.S. Coin No. 85

Good   Fine   Ex-Fine

U.S. Coin No. 86 Gold

Good	Fine	Ex-Fine

U.S. Coin No. 87

Good	Fine	Ex-Fine

U.S. Coin Nos. 88 and 96

Good   Fine   Ex-Fine

U.S. Coin Nos. 89, 90, and 105

Good   Fine   Ex-Fine

Good   Fine   Ex-Fine

U.S. Coin Nos. 92 and 100

Good   Fine   Ex-Fine

U.S. Coin Nos. 93 and 101

Good   Fine   Ex-Fine

U.S. Coin Nos. 94, 102, and 107

Good   Fine   Ex-Fine

U.S. Coin Nos. 95 and 104

| Good | Fine | Ex-Fine |

U. S. Coin No. 97

| Good | Fine | Ex-Fine |

U.S. Coin Nos. 98 and 106

Good   Fine   Ex-Fine

U.S. Coin Nos. 103 and 108

Good   Fine   Ex-Fine

U.S. Coin No. 105

Good   Fine   Ex-Fine

U.S. Coin Nos. 109 and 110

Good   Fine   Ex-Fine

U.S. Coin Nos. 111, 112, and 113

Good   Fine   Ex-Fine

U.S. Coin Nos. 114, 115, and 116

Good   Fine   Ex-Fine

CHAPTER IX

COUNTERFEIT AND UNAUTHORIZED COINS

"Whoever fraudulently alters, defaces, mutilates, impairs, diminishes, falsifies, scales, or lightens any of the coins coined at the mints of the United States, or any foreign coins which are by law made current or are in actual use or circulation as money within the United States; or—

"Whoever fraudently possesses, passes, utters, publishes, or sells, or attempts to pass, utter, publish, or sell, or bring into the United States, any such coin, knowing the same to be altered, defaced, mutilated, impaired, diminished, falsified, scaled, or lightened—

Shall be fined not more than $2,000 or imprisoned not more than five years, or both."

From Chapter 17, Mutilation, Diminution and Falsification of Coins, Title 18, U.S. Code, Section 331

The Act of July 16, 1951, amended this section, making it applicable to minor coins (five-cent and one-cent pieces), and to the fraudulent alteration of coins.

Definitions

An Authorized Coin

An authorized coin of the United States is one purposely struck within federal minting facilities; in accordance with the prevailing coinage act at the date of issue; of legal weight and composition, duly accounted for in the production records of the mint and by authority of the Mint Director.

An Unauthorized Coin

A coin of a likeness and similitude of an authorized coin, produced or caused to exist under any circumstance other than the conditions provided for an authorized coin, is an unauthorized coin and subject to confiscation by the federal government. It may be classified under any of the following:

A Counterfeit Coin

An imitation coin fabricated in the semblance of a genuine coin. It may be cast, die struck, engraved or an electrotype, of a base metal, an alloy identical to the genuine; an alloy unlike the genuine, or of a purer metal with a fineness in excess of that specified for the prototype. It may also be of a material other than metal but of a size and appearance resembling the genuine. It may be plated or unplated.

An Altered Coin

A genuine coin changed in any degree to resemble a genuine coin of exceptional value—having been produced or caused to exist under unusual circumstances. It may have the qualifying feature added by applying one lifted from a lesser specimen and "laid on" by any method of adhesion; engraving or re-engraving; "chasing" an existing feature to resemble another, and building the desired feature through an electrotype process.

It may have the disqualifying feature removed by etching, abrasive reduction, cutting, grinding or building sufficient extra material in the existing feature by electrotyping and then re-engraving; chasing or stamping the desired element.

A lightened or diminished unauthorized coin may have arrived at that condition by deliberate transfer of its precious metal through an electrotyping process; by "shaving" the high points; by direct removal in larger quantities through drilling and filling certain areas; or by removing the inner contents and replacing with a baser metal.

It may be a conversion from two genuine coins, having the obverse or reverse of a similar but different coin.

A Cast Counterfeit

This is a product of the oldest form of coin uniformity. It is literally molded in sand and cast, as in any other molten metal process, with the exception of the "lost wax" process. This differs only in the method used to "force" the liquefied elements deeper into the impression, giving the finished coin a sharper appearance. These pieces are detectable with an ordinary magnifying glass and close examination in confined areas where it would be difficult to "buff" or smooth away the sandy or pitted marks in the surface. Usually there is an indication of a flash line around the edge where the upper and lower halves of the mold did not completely unite. On coins with a reeded edge, this line is evident in the "valleys" between the reedings.

Modern technology has developed surprising improvements in pressure casting and, considering the amount of money involved in selling perfect specimens of a high-value coin, it is profitable to employ all finishing processes that will result in a better product.

An Electrotype Counterfeit

Electrotype reproductions have been made under legitimate conditions for the purpose of exhibit or federal coin cabinet specimens, but the same process has been used to produce illegal specimens also.

An impression of one side is made in a wax cake under pressure. The impression is coated with "black lead" and suspended in a bath of copper sulphate. Through an electroplating period a hairline impression is reproduced on a copper shell from the wax mold. When the required thickness has been achieved, the wax is melted away, leaving a finely detailed "copy" of the original in the form of a copper or silver dish.

This operation is repeated for the other side of the coin providing two "dished" or panlike halves that are ultimately joined together by whatever means the artisan finds appropriate. Usually these pieces are filled with lead or a similarly heavy metal to satisfy the weight of the original. Counterfeits produced by this method are extremely fine specimens and desirable in any case, but the joint between the two halves can be detected under a glass.

Die-Struck Counterfeits

A counterfeit made by the use of matched dies is difficult at best for anyone but an expert to detect, especially when the dies are made by skilled tool and die makers. Many of the unauthorized coins circulating today are die struck under ideal conditions. However, there are simple and metallurgical tests that will "unmask" these pieces.

Detecting
Altered Coins

A high-value coin with all the attributes of a genuine coin should still be subjected to close examination—especially if its qualifying feature is one capable of being applied, engraved, chased, or removed.

Example: If the coin in question is valued for the presence of a particular mint mark, examine that mark closely with a rather strong magnifying glass or stereoscope. If it is a "lay-on" lifted from a coin bearing the desired mint mark, it will probably show dark edges around the configuration of the letter (or in the case of a numeral, in the date). Under a glass these edges will also appear ragged and foreign. If so, it is undoubtedly a stranger.

If the general outline of the mark (or numeral) is not dark and appears to blend with the surface, examine the area within one or two millimeters of the edge with lighting from an angle just above the level of the coin. If the surface appears "dished" or concaved, the mark is probably the result of "chasing" or "pushing" the existing metal into the desired shape of the mark or numeral. Chasing is an old art but a skilled metalworker in that particular science can create masterpieces almost undetectable.

Dates are the likeliest of all to be tampered with. Here, it is of utmost importance that an original or similar copy be available in order to compare the numerals. If the qualifying date should happen to be 1914 or any combination of numerals involving 1, gauge the space between the 1 and the numerals on either side. If it is an altered coin, this space will be excessive and the surface will show "tool" or abrasion marks. If the key number is a 6 or an 8, examine the area for "chasing." A 6 can be chased from the numerals 3, 5, 8, 9, and 0 with ease. The others require some extra attention.

In cases involving the absence of a mint mark, numeral, or symbol in the design, look for a depressed area where that particular mark would normally be. Wearing down with fine emery dust or a jeweler's grinding tool will show when the coin is rotated under a glass with a reflecting light slightly above the level of the working surface.

Lightened or diminished coins are not the easiest to discover. This will require weighing, as do all the others, and authentication by X-ray spectrograph. However, there are times when a small drilled opening can be detected between the circumscribed lettering and the border, or in the valleys between the reedings. This opening may or may not be covered with the dominating metal, but any drilling into the center will have disturbed the facing surfaces of the reedings, which is hard to cover up. Coins diminished by an electrotyping process must be both weighed and also measured with good vernier-calipers.

Counterfeit and Unauthorized Coins.

The following unauthorized coins are known to exist in quantity and are listed by denomination, date, description, and chief illegal property. The absence of a date or denomination from this list by no means implies a coin is genuine.

Descriptions of known counterfeit and unauthorized coins were provided by the United States Secret Service; the American Numismatic Association Certification Service; and Don Taxay in his work *Counterfeit, Mis-struck and Official U.S. Coins.*

Early and Private Coinage

1616	Bermuda 12 Pence (Sommers)	Copperplated/lead base
1652	Pine-Tree Shilling (Mass.)	Silver-plated base metal
1652	Pine-Tree Shilling (Mass.)	3 pence, cast base metal
1652	Oak-Tree Shilling (Mass.)	Silver-plated base metal
1652	NE Shilling (Mass.)	Silver-plated base metal
1653	Willow-Tree Shilling	Silver-plated base metal
1776	New Hampshire Half Cent	Cast copper/counterfeit
1776	Continental Dollar	Cast pewter/base metal
1776	Pine-Tree Copper (Mass.)	Cast copper/counterfeit
1783	Nova Constellatio Cent	Cast copper/silver-plated
1787	Brasher's Doubloon	Cast base metal/counterfeit pattern
1787	Brasher's Doubloon	Cast base metal/gold-plated
1787	Fugio Cent	Copperplated/basé metal
1787	Fugio Cent	Cast copper/counterfeit
1788	Massachusetts Penny	Copperplated/cast base metal
1788	Massachusetts One Cent	Die-struck counterfeit
1788	Massachusetts Half Cent	Die-struck counterfeit
1792	Birch Cent	Copperplated base metal
1792	Washington Half-Dollar	Copper electrotype
1792	Washington Half-Dollar	Cast base metal/copper; silver-plated
1849	Norris, Greig, and Norris	($5) Cast base metal/gold-plated
1849	Oregon Exchange	($5) Cast base metal/gold-plated
1861	Confederate State Dime	Die-struck/silver planchet

Half Cent

1793	Half Cent	Cast copper counterfeit
1793	Half Cent	Copper electrotype
1794	Half Cent	Copper electrotype
1796	Half Cent	Copper electrotype
1796	Half Cent	Cast copper
1796	Half Cent	Altered coin/pole removed
1811	Half Cent	Copper electrotype
1811	Half Cent	Cast bronze
1831	Half Cent	Copper electrotype
1836	Half Cent	Copper electrotype
1840 to 1849	Half Cent	Copper electrotypes and some specimens of Cast copper
1852	Half Cent	Copper electrotype

One Cent, Large

1795	One Cent, Large	Copper electrotype
1795	One Cent, Large	Cast copper
1799	One Cent, Large	Cast base metal
1799	One Cent, Large	Altered date/last digit
1802	One Cent, Large	Copper electrotype
1803	One Cent, Large	Copper electrotype
1804	One Cent, Large	Copperplated
1815	One Cent, Large	Plated cast base metal
1815	One Cent, Large	Electrotype
1823	One Cent, Large	Cast copper/buffed
1851	One Cent, Large	Cast copper

One Cent, Small

1856	Flying Eagle (Pattern)	Altered date/from "1858"
1856	Flying Eagle (Pattern)	Cast base metal
1856	Flying Eagle (Pattern)	Die-struck counterfeit
1856	Flying Eagle	Altered from 1858/chased "6"
1858	Flying Eagle	Fake proof/treated and buffed
1877	Indian Head	Re-engraved last digit
1877	Indian Head	Second "8" chased to "7" from "1887"
1877	Indian Head	Cast bronze/careless casting
1909-S	Lincoln Head (VDB)	Altered "1909"/mint letter laid on
1909-S	Lincoln Head (VDB)	Altered "1909"/chased mint letter
1909-S	Lincoln Head (VDB)	Die-struck/almost perfect
1909-S	Indian Head	Cast bronze/counterfeit
1909-S	Indian Head	Letter s added
1913-D	Lincoln Head	Cast copper-poor

Counterfeit and Unauthorized Coins Continued

One Cent, Small Continued

1914-D	Lincoln Head	Mint letter chased from s
1914-D	Lincoln Head	Mint letter d laid on
1914-D	Lincoln Head (VDB) Obv.	Altered date/from 1944-d
1914-D	Lincoln Head	Altered date/from 1911-d
1914-D	Lincoln Head	Cast bronze/from original, rough
1922	Lincoln Head (Broken d)	Altered/mint letter d removed
1922	Lincoln Head (Broken d)	Altered/last digit chased from "1923"
1922	Lincoln Head (Broken d)	Cast copper/sharp
1922	Lincoln Head (Broken d)	Last digit laid on/altered "1920"
1931-S	Lincoln Head	Altered from "1930-s"
1931-S	Lincoln Head	Mint letter s laid on 1931
1950	Lincoln Head Proof	Fake highly polished regular cent
1955	Double-struck Lincoln	Die-struck/almost perfect/import
1960	Small-Date Lincoln	"960" are chased/"1" untouched

Two-Cent Piece

1864	Small Motto Two Cents	Cast copper/highly buffed

Three-Cent Piece (Nickel)

1865	Three Cents	Die-struck/German nickel-silver
1866	Three Cents	Die-struck/German nickel-silver
1877	Three Cents Proof	Cast/altered/plated and buffed

Three Cents (Silver)

1852	Three Cents	Cast silver
1855	Three Cents	Cast silver
1855	Three Cents	Cast silver-plated
1860	Three Cents	Die-struck/German nickel-silver
1861	Three Cents	

Five Cents

All dates have been known to be counterfeited but detectable

1870	Shield Five Cents	Die-struck/German nickel-silver
1871	Shield Five Cents	Die-struck/German nickel-silver
1875	Shield Five Cents	Die-struck/German nickel-silver
1878	Shield Five Cents	Cast/German nickel-silver

Counterfeit and Unauthorized Coins Continued

Five Cents Continued

1885	Liberty Five Cents	Cast base metal/plated
1885	Liberty Five Cents	Cast base metal/plated
1900	Liberty Five Cents	s added
1912-D	Liberty Five Cents	Mint letter "D" laid on
1912-S	Liberty Five Cents	Mint letter "S" laid on
1913	Liberty Five Cents (UNA)	Altered from "1903"/cast base metal
1913	Liberty Five Cents (UNA)	Altered coin/second "1" laid on
1914-D	Indian Head Five Cents	Altered coin/mint letter D laid on
1937	Indian Head Five Cents	
	Three-Legged Buffalo	Altered/right front leg removed
1918/17	Indian Head Five Cents	Altered coin/numeral "7" chased
1926-S	Indian Head Five Cents	s added
1939-D	Jefferson Five Cents	Die-struck/counterfeit (see page 124)
1950-D	Jefferson Five Cents	Die-struck/counterfeit (see page 125)
1944	Jefferson Five Cents	Mint letter P removed
1944	Jefferson Five Cents	Cast silver alloy
1950-D	Jefferson Five Cents	D added

Half Dime

1796	Draped Bust Half Dime	Cast copper/plated
1796	Draped Bust Half Dime	Copper electrotype-plated
1796	Draped Bust Half Dime	Silver electrotype
1797	Draped Bust Half Dime	Silver electrotype
1800	Draped Bust Half Dime	Cast silver/alloyed
1849-O	Liberty Seated Half Dime	Mint letter o laid on
1838	Liberty Seated Half Dime	Cast planchet/hand engraved

Dimes

1797	Draped Bust Dime	Silver electrotype
1798	Draped Bust Dime	Silver electrotype
1798	Draped Bust Dime	Cast base metal/plated
1871-CC	Seated Liberty Dime	Cast copper/silver-plated
1889-S	Seated Liberty Dime	Cast silver alloy
1890	Seated Liberty Dime	Silver electrotype
1891	Seated Liberty Dime	Cast silver
1892	Liberty Head (Barber) Dime	Cast silver
1892	Liberty Head (Barber) Dime	Cast copper/silver-plated
1894-S	Liberty Head (Barber) Dime	Cast silver alloy
1907	Liberty Head (Barber) Dime	Cast silver
1911	Liberty Head (Barber) Dime	Cast silver
1921-D	Liberty Head (Barber) Dime	Cast silver alloy

Counterfeit and Unauthorized Coins Continued

Dimes Continued

1913	Liberty Head (M) Dime	Altered from 1943 Dime
1916-D	Liberty Head (M) Dime	Re-engraved feathers in the helmet
1916-D	Liberty Head (M) Dime	Mint letter D laid on
1916-D	Liberty Head (M) Dime	Mint letter D/chased from letter s
1916-D	Liberty Head (M) Dime	Altered coin/chased 1926-D
1916-D	Liberty Head (M) Dime	A clad process with reeded edge
1916-D	Liberty Head (M) Dime	Die-struck/almost perfect
1916-D	Liberty Head (M) Dime	"1916" genuine/electrotype D
1916-D	Liberty Head (M) Dime	Cast-silver counterfeit
1921-D	Liberty Head (M) Dime	Mint letter D laid on
1921-D	Liberty Head (M) Dime	Numeral "4" chased to numeral "2"
1923-D	Liberty Head (M) Dime	Die-struck counterfeit
1931-D	Liberty Head (M) Dime	Mint letter D laid on
1942-D41	Liberty Head (M) Dime	Cast-silver counterfeit

Twenty Cents

1877	Liberty Seated (20¢)	Cast Counterfeit

Quarter Dollar

1916	Washington (25¢)	Altered coin/from "1946"
1932-S	Washington (25¢)	Mint letter s laid on
1932-S	Washington (25¢)	Cast silver/sand finish
1932-D	Washington (25¢)	Cast silver/sand finish
1853	Liberty Seated (25¢)	Altered from "1858"
1853	Liberty Seated (25¢)	Silver-plated electrotype
1853	Liberty Seated (25¢)	Counterfeit counterstamp/fleur-de-lis of Puerto Rico
1853	Liberty Seated (25¢)	Cast silver
1854	Liberty Seated (25¢)	Counterfeit counterstamp/fleur-de-lis of Puerto Rico
1858	Liberty Seated (25¢)	Cast silver
1861-S	Liberty Seated (25¢)	Cast silver
1872-CC	Liberty Seated (25¢)	Cast silver/dull finish
1877-S	Liberty Seated (25¢)	Cast silver
1896-S	Liberty Head (B) 25¢	Cast silver
1909-O	Liberty Head (B) 25¢	Cast silver
1919-S	Standing Liberty (25¢)	Cast silver/flat details
1932-S	Washington (25¢)	Letter s chased
1932-D	Washington (25¢)	Letter D added
1932-D	Washington (25¢)	Letter D chased and plated
1936-D	Washington (25¢)	Cast silver/buffed to appear cir.
1964-S	Washington (25¢)	Mint letter s/added
1964	Washington (25¢)	Cast silver alloy
1964	Washington (25¢)	Plated and polished
1965	Washington (25¢)	Silver-plated
1967	Washington (25¢)	Cast silver/almost pure
1967	Washington (25¢)	Copper plated/offered as trial piece

Half-Dollar

1794	Flowing Hair (50¢)	Electrotype/plated
1794	Flowing Hair (50¢)	Silver electrotype

Half-Dollar Continued

1796	Draped Bust (50¢)	Silver electrotype
1826	Liberty Cap (50¢)	Silver plated/copper planchet
1830	Liberty Cap (50¢)	Die-struck/German nickel-silver
1832	Liberty Cap (50¢)	Die-struck/German nickel-silver
1833	Liberty Cap (50¢)	Die-struck/German nickel-silver
1835	Liberty Cap (50¢)	Die-struck/German nickel-silver
1836	Liberty Cap (50¢)	Die-struck/cast planchet
1837	Liberty Cap (50¢)	Die-struck/German nickel-silver
1837	Liberty Cap (50¢)	Cast silver alloy
1838	Liberty Cap (50¢)	Die-struck/German nickel-silver
1840	Liberty Seated (50¢)	Die-struck/German nickel-silver
1858	Liberty Seated (50¢)	Cast silver
1858	Liberty Seated (50¢)	Cast silver
1861	Liberty Seated (50¢)	Cast silver
1873	Liberty Seated (50¢)	Cast silver alloy
1876	Liberty Seated (50¢)	Cast silver
1877	Liberty Seated (50¢)	Cast silver
1878-CC	Liberty Seated (50¢)	Cast silver
1878-S	Liberty Seated (50¢)	Cast silver
1892	Columbian Expo. (50¢)	Proof/actually high polish
1892	Columbian Expo. (50¢)	Cast silver alloy
1918	**Walking Liberty (50¢)**	**Cast silver**
1921-D	**Walking Liberty (50¢)**	**Cast silver**
1921-D	**Walking Liberty (50¢)**	**Cast silver**
1938-D	**Walking Liberty (50¢)**	Mint letter D laid on
1873	**Liberty Seated (50¢)**	**Cast base metal/silver-plated**
1914	**Franklin (50¢)**	**Altered coin/from "1944"**
1964	Kennedy Head (50¢)	Cast silver alloy
1965	Kennedy Head (50¢)	Silver-plated
1967	Kennedy Head (50¢)	Copper-plated, offered as a trial piece

One Dollar

1901	Liberty Head (M) ($1)	Cast counterfeit/proof like field
1928-P	Peace Dollar	Mint letter removed
1879	Liberty Head (M) ($1)	Cast counterfeit/almost pure silver
1879-CC	Liberty Head (M) ($1)	Cast counterfeit/satin buff
1879-CC	Liberty Head (M) ($1)	Genuine coin/mint letters CC laid on
1885-CC	Liberty Head (M) ($1)	Cast-silver counterfeit
1889-CC	Liberty Head (M) ($1)	Cast-silver counterfeit
1889-CC	Liberty Head (M) ($1)	Genuine coin/mint letters CC laid on
1892-S	Liberty Head (M) ($1)	Genuine coin/mint letter S laid on
1893-S	Liberty Head (M) ($1)	Genuine coin/mint letter S laid on
1804	Draped Bust ($1)	Silver electrotype
1804	Draped Bust ($1)	Copper electrotype/silver-plated
1804	Draped Bust ($1)	Cast silver

Counterfeit and Unauthorized Coins Continued

One Dollar Continued

1804	Draped Bust ($1)	Genuine coin/altered last digit
1804	Draped Bust ($1)	Genuine coin/electrotype numeral "4"
1874-CC	Trade Dollar	Cast silver alloy
1885-CC	Morgan Head	Cast silver alloy
1893-CC	Morgan Head	Altered from 1898-s
1903-S	Liberty Head (M) ($1)	Genuine coin/mint letter s laid on

Gold Counterfeit and Unauthorized Coins

One Dollar

1852	Liberty Head Type I	Cast gold
1852 to 1854	Type I Liberty Head	Cast gold/high purity
1859	Indian Head	Cast pure gold
1859	Indian Head	Cast pure gold
1868	Type III Indian Head	Cast gold/high purity
1868	Type III Indian Head	Cast copper planchet/gold-plated

Quarter Eagle ($2.50)

1808	Type III Liberty Cap	Cast gold
1843-C	Type VI Coronet	Cast gold
1843-C	Type VI Coronet	Cast copper planchet/gold-plated
1843	Type VI Coronet	Cast gold
1911	Indian Head	Cast gold alloy
1928-D	Indian Head	Cast gold alloy
1929-D	Indian Head	Cast gold alloy

Three Dollar ($3.00)

1855	Indian Head	Cast gold alloy
1865	Indian Head	Cast *pure* gold
1878	Indian Head	Cast gold alloy
1866	Coronet	Cast/electroplate
1908-S	Indian Head	Cast gold
1908-S	Indian Head	Cast copper planchet/gold-plated
1806	Liberty Cap/HE	Cast gold alloy
1889	Type VI Coronet	Cast gold
1889	Type VI Coronet	Cast gold/low grade
1908	Standing Liberty	Good gold cast
1908-S	Standing Liberty	Good gold cast
1908	Standing Liberty	Cast gold—pure
1908-S	Standing Liberty	s laid on

Counterfeit and Unauthorized Coins Continued

Half Eagle ($5.00)

1803	Type II Liberty Cap	Gold-plated brass
1803	Type II Liberty Cap	Cast gold
1842	Type VI Coronet	Cast gold
1844	Type VI Coronet	Cast gold
1846	Type VI Coronet	Cast gold
1846-D	Type VI Coronet	Altered date/last digit "chased"
1908-S	Indian Head	Cast gold
1908-S	Indian Head	Cast copper planchet/gold-plated
1909-O	Indian Head	Genuine coin/mint letter o laid on
1915-D	Indian Head	Cast-gold counterfeit

Eagle ($10.00)

1889	Type VI Coronet	Cast gold
1889	Type VI Coronet	Cast gold/low grade
1916	Type VI Indian Head	Cast gold
1933	Indian Head	Cast gold

Double Eagle ($20.00)

1908	Standing Liberty	Cast gold alloy
1908-S	Standing Liberty	Good gold with s laid on
1890-CC	Coronet	Cast gold alloy
1885	Coronet	Mint mark removed

CHAPTER X

THE UNITED STATES SECRET SERVICE

This bureau of the Treasury Department is the oldest law-enforcement agency in the federal government and has headquarters in Washington, D.C., and field offices throughout the U.S. It was established in 1865 for the express purpose of checking widespread counterfeit and alteration of the nation's currency.

The duties of the Secret Service are described in the United States Code, Title 18, Section 3056. In addition to protection of the President, the President-elect, the Vice President, the Vice President-elect, their families, and related responsibilities, its functions are:

The detection and arrest of persons engaged in counterfeiting, forgery, or alteration of currency, checks, bonds, and other obligations of the United States and of foreign governments, including violations concerning the manufacturing, sale, and use of tokens, slugs, paper, or other things similar in size and shape to any of the lawful coins or other currency of the United States.

Counterfeit and Forgery

An authorized coin of the United States is an obligation of the United States, and any unauthorized reproduction as defined in the United States Code is considered unlawful and subject to the penalties described in violations by classification.

Sections from Title 18 of the United States Code will familiarize the reader with the requirements of the code, thereby avoiding direct or indirect involvement in an illegal act pertaining to the coinage of the United States. (See Appendix for law and penalties pertaining to counterfeiting and forgery, mutilation, diminution, and falsification of U.S. Coins.)

You and the Secret Service

A statement by the director of the United States Secret Service to the effect that an informed public is a strong foe of the counterfeiter is backed by constant efforts of the Secret Service to educate the public on the detection of counterfeit money and the steps to take when a piece of questionable currency is circulated:

1—DO NOT RETURN IT TO THE PASSER—unless it is detected at the time · of exchange at a bank or cashier's window.

2—DELAY THE PASSER—Use any reasonable excuse to delay the passer until help can be summoned, such as a store manager or person of authority to whom you can relate the situation without causing the passer to notice. Note his physical appearance, license, etc.

3—TELEPHONE THE NEAREST POLICE PRECINCT OR HEADQUARTERS. Explain the conditions under which you received the counterfeit, give a description of the passer, his car, or any identifying qualities.

4—WRITE YOUR NAME OR INITIALS AND THE DATE—IN INK—ON THE FACE OF PAPER CURRENCY—Ask the responding officer for identification (this is not considered offensive to a police officer). Ask for a receipt before surrendering the counterfeit—but under no circumstance surrender it to anyone other than a recognized police officer or bona-fide representative of the United States Secret Service.

A cooperating citizen is never subjected to publicity, embarrassment, or inconvenienced in any way as a result of performing his civic duty.

CHAPTER XI

VERIFICATION TESTS

There are two categories into which it is possible to classify an unauthorized coin: the nonprofessional and the professional, or, if preferable, the bad and the good.

In the first instance, the coin is usually the product of an unskilled person, produced either as a gag or perhaps in a deliberate effort to defraud. In either event, the workmanship is poor and instantly detectable as is the composition (if counterfeit), which in practically every case is lead or a similar base metal. These pieces are short-lived and rarely found anywhere but in a keepsake box in an old desk drawer.

The good professional coins are something else. These pieces are painstakingly accurate and most difficult to distinguish from the genuine. In many cases the appearance is much better than the mint product. They are almost always the work of an organized process before which the manufacturer studied both the probable market and the coins most in demand. Good research is a basic requirement to produce unauthorized coins of a type that will be acceptable without too much dickering and horse trading.

It is with the good unauthorized coins that the following tests have been used and found to be accurate to within one percent of the pieces tested, that one percent being of the electrotype variety. These were finally exposed, however, by a spectrograph test.

If the authenticity of the coin in question is still undetermined after these simple tests, try the chemical test, but in any case, any questionable coin should be subjected to the specific-gravity test.

Visual Comparison

Always compare a suspected fake with a similar coin known to be genuine, and in a comparable condition. Examine the lettering, the date, the border, and edge. Look for fallen or flat configurations on the suspect. The reedings will be uneven and irregular.

Touch Comparison

Lay both coins on the same surface for approximately one minute to allow them time to assume the same temperature. Pick one up in each hand and rub the tip of the index finger back and forth under a very light pressure. The counterfeit will often feel greasy.

Close the fist over each coin and hold for a few seconds. The bad, or unauthorized, piece will seem to generate more heat than the genuine.

Sound Test

Place the questionable coin on the ball of the left index finger and strike it gently with the good coin. Reverse the pieces and strike the good coin with the suspected fake. The genuine will have a much higher and melodious tone. Even if the coin being tested is counterfeited from the same composition, the sound will be less lively. The tone of an altered coin is slightly more difficult to distinguish.

Check these areas for differences between the two coins. Start with the left edge of the design and work around and down to the date before concentrating on the main device. Observe the areas between the border and the inscription as well as those between the letters. On a coin of genuine character, the surface in these places will be free of any rough or metallic obstructions. Look at the normally sharp points on the edges of all lettering. A counterfeit will show them to be nubbed or slightly rounded. Check the diameter by holding pieces together.

Chemical Test

The chemicals involved in this test are not completely harmless and certain precautions should be taken to protect the working-surface area. Since the amount of the formula required to arrive at a conclusion is so small, it would be advisable to purchase the formulas in minimal quantities along with small laboratory dishes and counteracting wash.

Testing A Silver Coin		Testing A Gold Coin	
Formula:		Formula:	
Silver nitrate	12 grains	Nitric acid	6½ drams
Nitric acid	15 drops	Muratic acid	¼ dram
Distilled water	½ ounce	Distilled water	5 drams

Chemical Test

Using a small cake candle, let one drop of wax fall on the reeded edge of the coin. When it has set, remove the wax from a valley between two of the reedings with a needle, making sure not to disturb the wax on the outer surface of the reedings or the edge of the coin.

Stand the coin upright between two small objects sufficiently heavy to hold the coin steady. Place a small adjustable magnifier close enough to bring the exposed valley into sharp focus.

When the eye becomes accustomed to the selected spot, apply a touch of the proper formula to the unwaxed valley. If the surface darkens, it is the composition represented.

Rinse the coin immediately in a counteracting solution of ammonia or baking soda. Remove the excess wax and wipe with the small lens cloth provided with the kit.

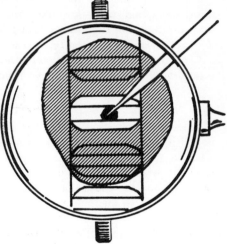

Specific Gravity Test

The density, or thickness, of United States coins varies according to the compactness of the molecular structure of each of the five metals used to produce them. Just as a one-inch cube of sponge would differ in gravitational pull from a one-inch cube of concrete, so would equal cubes of zinc and gold. For this reason the weight of a coin is never sufficient to determine its authenticity. Furthermore, a circulated coin would obviously be lighter than an uncirculated specimen of the same coin.

While the loss of metal may affect the mass weight of a coin, nothing can wear on its density. Any portion of a metal will show the same specific-gravity quotient as any other part of the same metal, making density the key element to the composition. Comparison with an element of a known standard—in this case, water—is the common practice.

Specific gravity is the number of times a volume of metal is heavier than an equal volume of water.

In performing a specific gravity test, the weight of a coin in water subtracted from its dry air weight will give the weight of the water displaced. The weight of the coin in air is divided by the displacement weight. The quotient carried to no more than three places after the decimal is the specific gravity value of the coin.

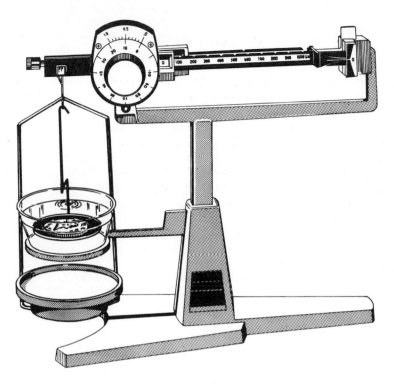

Special Equipment

Determining the weight and specific gravity of a coin is by no means a complicated procedure and in the absence of specialized equipment the student or non-professional will find it appropriate to improvise the necessary accessories. The equipment should be of reasonable sensitivity preferably designed to give the weight in grains without the necessity of mathematical conversion.

Implementation is not recommended for the professional numismatist or in cases involving findings of legal consequence. Here the situation calls for inexpensive but highly specialized instruments intended solely for the execution of weight check and specific gravity tests. Such scales relieve the operator of the need for more than a minimal knowledge of weights and measures so long as he is capable of following step-by-step procedural instructions.

Paramount International Coin Corporation of Englewood, Ohio, is the sole distributor of the 3100 Numiscale designed especially for professional and nonprofessional numismatists. It operates on a highly sensitive dial principal rather than a sliding poise and can be operated by anyone capable of reading an instruction sheet.

The 3100 has a capacity of 3,100 grains and a sensitivity of 0.1 grains, with beam graduations of 2,000 grains x 1,000 grains and 1,000 grains x 100 grains. Dial and vernier readings are 100 grains x 0.1 grain.

Specific Gravity Values for All
United States Coinage

While the specific-gravity reading of a coin is merely a means of identifying its density—and will in a majority of cases establish the authenticity of a coin—it should not be considered conclusive in a coin of extremely high value. Counterfeit coins have been known to contain alloys that purposely raise the weight to one of legal requirement and at the same time provide that coin with a density not unlike the genuine. Example: The specific-gravity numeral for a Lincoln Cent of 95% copper, 2½% tin, and 2½% zinc is so close to that of a Lincoln Cent with a composition of 95% copper and 5% zinc that it would be difficult to detect a 1909-SVDB struck on a planchet of the new composition from an original of the old composition. For that reason the present one-cent pieces referred to in the unauthorized section may show specific-gravity numerals close enough to appear genuine even though of unauthorized composition.

The specific-gravity quotients* in the following table are official and should be used exclusive of all others in a specific-gravity test.

Unalloyed Metals	Specific-Gravity Quotient
Gold	19.32+
Silver	10.49+
Copper	8.96+
Nickel	8.90
Tin	7.298
Manganese	7.3
Zinc	7.13

Alloyed Metals	Specific-Gravity Quotient
95% copper, 2½% zinc, 2½% tin	8.87270
95% copper, 5% zinc	8.8685
75% copper, 25% nickel	8.945
10% copper, 90% silver	10.337
60% copper, 40% silver (1965 Half-Dollar)	9.572
75% copper, 25% nickel clad on a solid copper core. (1965 to date)	8.955
88% copper, 12% nickel (Flying Eagle Cent)	8.95
25% copper, 75% silver	10.1075
107.6 parts copper/892.4 parts silver	10.3253
Steel one-cent piece, zinc coated (1943)	7.8 + or −
56% copper, 35% silver, 9% manganese wartime silver five-cent composition	9.346+
Gold coins prior to 1860	17.3
Gold coins after 1860	17.2

* Due to probable chemical imbalance in one or more alloys—a plus or minus .5 variation in a reading is acceptable.

Authentication Services

Under the law, any person in possession of a coin known to be unlawful is required to surrender that coin forthwith to the Director of the United States Secret Service through the nearest office of that agency. This applies to appraisers, insurance agents, bankers, attorneys, and police officers who may on occasion discover such an item in an estate, collection or in the effects of anyone under their jurisdiction. It may not be passed, returned to the original owner, or destroyed once its illegal position has been determined. Anyone held accountable for the coin in question can satisfy the claimant, estate, or original owner with a receipt tendered by the United States Secret Service when the coin is duly surrendered.

In the event a coin is determined to be counterfeit, altered, or suspected of being unauthorized for any reason, it may be submitted to the United States Secret Service for authentication. If it proves to be an unlawful coin, a receipt will be issued and the coin confiscated. Should it be declared genuine, however, it will be returned to the sender. The area of this service is limited to whether or not the coin is legal in accordance with the coinage act governing the specification for that particular coin. The Secret Service will not pass on the numismatic merits of a collector's item and whether it is, or is not, a coin of any other than its intended value.

Coins as collector's items, or those represented as collector's items, may be submitted to professional authentication laboratories equipped to provide this specialized service. It is therefore advisable to submit any coin of particular value to one of these laboratories for verification before buying or selling at any value over face denomination. The firms will, in each case, return the coin with an authentication that can testify to its status. This authentication warrant should accompany the coin throughout all transfer actions that involve change of ownership.

1. Office of the Director
    United States Secret Service
    Washington, D.C. 20226

2. American Numismatic Association
        Certification Service
    Charles Hoskins, Director
    Box 87
    Benjamin Franklin Station
    Washington, D.C.

    NOTE: Please write for instructions
    on correct procedure for mailing
    coins to assure safe delivery.

APPENDIX

Counterfeiting and Forgery

Title 18, U.S. Code, Section 485

Coins or bars: Whoever falsely makes, forges, or counterfeits any coin or bar in resemblance or similitude of any coin of a denomination higher than 5 cents or any gold or silver bar coined or stamped at any mint or assay office of the United States, or in resemblance or similitude of any foreign gold or silver coin current in the United States or in actual use and circulation as money within the United States; or

Whoever passes, utters, publishes, sells, possesses, or brings into the United States any false, forged, or counterfeit coin or bar, knowing the same to be false, forged, or counterfeit, with intent to defraud any body politic or corporate, or any person, or attempts the commission of any offense described in this paragraph—

Shall be fined not more than $5,000 or imprisoned not more than fifteen years, or both.

Section 486

Uttering coins of gold, silver or other metal: Whoever, except as authorized by law, makes or utters or passes, or attempts to utter or pass, any coins of gold or silver or other metal, or alloys or metals, intended for use as current money, whether in resemblance of coins of the United States or of foreign countries, or of original design, shall be fined not more than $3,000 or imprisoned not more than five years, or both.

Section 487

Making or possessing counterfeit dies for coins: Whoever, without lawful authority, makes any die, hub, or mold, or any part thereof, either of steel or plaster, or any other substance, in likeness or similitude, as to the design or the inscription thereon, of any die, hub, or mold designated for the coining or making of any of the genuine gold, silver, nickel, bronze, copper, or other coins coined at the mints of the United States; or

Whoever, without lawful authority, possesses any such die, hub, or mold, or any part thereof, or permits the same to be used for or in aid of the counterfeiting of any such coins of the United States—

Shall be fined not more than $5,000 or imprisoned not more than fifteen years, or both.

> *Note:* The manufacture of a mold is one offense and the possession of such a mold is another; hence, under an indictment charging each of these offenses in a separate count, defendant could be convicted and sentenced on both counts.

Section 488

Making or possessing counterfeit dies for foreign coins: Whoever, within the United States, without lawful authority, makes any die, hub, or mold, or any part thereof, either of steel or of plaster, or of any other substance, in the likeness or similitude, as to the design or the inscription thereon, of any die, hub, or mold designated for the coining of the genuine coin of an foreign government; or

Whoever, without lawful authority, possesses any such die, hub, or mold, or any part thereof, or conceals, or knowingly suffers the same to be used for the counterfeiting of any foreign coin—

Shall be fined not more than $5,000 or imprisoned not more than five years, or both.

Section 489

Making or possessing likeness of coins: Whoever, within the United States, makes or brings therein from any foreign country, or possesses with intent to sell, give away, or in any manner use the same, except under the authority of the Secretary of the Treasury or other proper officer of the United States, any token, disk, or device in the likeness or similitude as to design, color, or the inscription thereon of any coin of the United States or of any foreign country issued as money, either under the authority of the United States or under the authority of any foreign government shall be fined not more than $100.

Section 490

Minor Coins: Whoever falsely makes, forges, or counterfeits any coin in the resemblance or similitude of any of the minor coins coined at the mints of the United States; or

Whoever passes, utters, publishes, or sells, or brings into the United States, or possesses any such false, forged, or counterfeit coin, with intent to defraud any person, shall be fined not more than $1,000 or imprisoned not more than three years, or both.

> *Note:* A coin is counterfeit when it, although originally a true coin, was punched and multilated, and base metal was used in replacing the portion removed; not so if it was merely punched without loss of original metal.

Section 491

Tokens or paper used as money: Whoever, being 18 years of age and over not lawfully authorized, makes, issues, or passes any coin, card, token, or device in metal, or its compounds, intended to be used as money, or whoever, being 18 years of age or over, with intent to fraud, makes, utters, inserts, or uses any card, token, slug, disk, device, paper, or other thing similar in size and shape to any of the lawful coins or other currency of the United States or any coin or other currency not legal tender in the United States, to procure anything of value, or the use or enjoyment of any property or service from any automatic merchandise vending machine, postage stamp machine turnstile, fare box, coin-box telephone, parking meter or other lawful receptacle, depository, or contrivance designed to receive or to be operated by lawful coins or other currency of the United States, shall be fined not more than $1,000 or imprisoned not more than one year, or both.

Whoever manufactures, sells, offers, or advertises for sale, or exposes or keeps with intent to furnish or sell any token, slug, disk, device, paper, or other thing similar in size and shape to any of the lawful coins or other currency of the United States, or any token, disk, paper, or other device issued or authorized in connection with rationing or food and fiber distribution by any agency of the United States, with knowledge or reason to believe that such tokens, slugs, disks, devices, papers, or other things are intended to be used unlawfully or fraudulently to procure anything of value, or the use or enjoyment of any property or service from any automatic merchandise vending machine, postage stamp machine, turnstile fare box, coin-box telephone, parking meter, or other lawful receptacle, depository, or contrivance designed to receive or to be operated by lawful coins or other currency of the United States shall be fined not more than $1000 or imprisoned not more than one year, or both.

Nothing contained in this section shall create immunity from criminal prosecution under the laws of any State, Commonwealth of Puerto Rico, territory, possession, or District of Columbia.

"Knowledge or reason to believe," within the meaning of paragraph (b) of this section, may be shown by proof that any law-enforcement officer has, prior to the commission of the offense with which the defendant is charged, informed the defendant that tokens, slugs, disks, or other devices of the kind manufactured, sold, offered, or advertised for sale by him or exposed or kept with intent to furnish or sell, are being used unlawfully or fraudulently to operate certain specified automatic merchandise vending machines, turnstiles, fare boxes, coin-box telephones, parking meters, or other receptacles, depositories, or contrivances, designed to receive or to be operated by lawful coins of the United States.

Section 492

Forfeiture of counterfeit paraphernalia: All counterfeits of any coins or obligations or other securities of the United States or of any foreign government, or any articles, devices, and other things made, possessed, or used in violation of this chapter . . . of this title, or any material or apparatus used or fitted or intended to be used, in the making of such counterfeits, articles, devices, or things, found in the possession of any person without authority from the Secretary of the Treasury or other proper officer, shall be forfeited to the United States.

Whoever, having the custody or control of any such counterfeits, material, apparatus, articles, devices, or other things, fails or refuses to surrender possession thereof upon request by any authorized agent of the Treasury Department, or other proper officer, shall be fined not more than $100 or imprisoned not more than one year, or both.

Whenever, except as hereinafter in this section provided, any person interested in any article, device, or other thing, or material or apparatus seized under this section files with the Secretary of the Treasury, before the disposition thereof, a petition for the remission or mitigation of such forfeiture, the Secretary of the Treasury, if he finds that such forfeiture was incurred without willful negligence or without any intention on the part of the petitioner to violate the law, or finds the existence of such mitigating circumstances as to justify the remission or the mitigation of such forfeiture, may remit or mitigate the forfeiture upon such terms as he deems reasonable and just.

Note: Seizure and forfeiture is not taking property without due process of law within the meaning of the Fifth Amendment to Constitution (Const. Amend. 5), since such coins were neither property nor the subject of property, but were products of felonious acts outside the law.

Nothing in this section authorizes the Secretary of the Treasury to return to a person from whom a coin was taken, the counterfeit or the value of the bullion it contained.

Treasury Department has the authority to determine when a coin is counterfeit, when unlawfully in the possession of a party from whom taken, and to forfeit it, and after forfeiture, to direct in what manner it should be disposed of, with no judicial condemnation being necessary.

BIBLIOGRAPHY

Belles, A. S., *Money, Banking, and Finance.* New York, American Book Company, 1903.

Brown, M. R., and Dunn, J. W., *A Guide to Grading of U. S. Coins.* Racine, Whitman Publishing Company, 1969.

Bullowa, David M., *Commemorative Coinage of the United States.* New York, The American Numismatic Society, 1938.

Chamberlain, C. C., and Reinfeld, F., *Coin Dictionary and Guide.* New York, Sterling Publishing Company, 1961.

Coin World, ed., *Coin Collecting for Fun and Profit.* New York, Arco Publishing Company, Inc., 1963.

Harris, R. P., *Pillars and Portraits.* New York, Bonanza Press, 1958.

Hetrich, George, and Guttag Julius, *Civil War Tokens and Tradesmen's Cards.* Stow, Mass., Alfred D. Hoch, 1968.

LaSeur, P., *Exchange Tables.* Montreal, John Lovell and Son, 1899.

Lindheim, Leon, *Facts and Fictions About Coins.* Cleveland, World Publishing Company, 1967.

Masters and Reinfeld, *Coinometry.* New York, Sterling Publishing Company, 1958.

Neuce, E., *Basic Knowledge for Coin Collectors.* Sidney, Ohio, Sidney Printing and Publishing Company, 1964.

Newman, E. P., and Bressert, K. E. *The Fantastic 1804 Dollar.* Racine, Wis., Whitman Publishing Company, 1962.

Rochette, E. C., *Medallic Portrait of John F. Kennedy.* Iola, Wisc., Krause Publications, Inc., 1966.

Sheldon, *Penny Whimsy.* New York, Harper and Row, Publishers, 1958.

Spadone, F. G., *Major Variety and Oddity Guide of United States Coinage.* Iola, Wisc., Krause Publications, Inc., 1967.

Stamp, J., *Papers on Gold and the Price Level.* London, P. S. King and Son, Ltd., 1931.

Taxay, Don, *Counterfeit, Mis-struck and Unofficial U.S. Coins.* New York, Arco Publishing Company, 1963.

Taxay, Don, *Illustrated History of U. S. Commemorative Coinage.* New York, Arco Publishing Company, 1967.

Taxay, Don, *U. S. Mint and Coinage*. New York, Arco Publishing Company, 1966.

U. S. Secret Service, *Know Your Money*. Washington, D. C., U. S. Government Printing Office, 1966.

U. S. Treasury Department, *Catalog of Coins, Medals, and Tokens*. Philadelphia, Philadelphia Mint Collection.

Yeoman, R. S., *A Catalog of Modern World Coins*. Racine, Wis., Western Publishing Company, 1970.

Yeoman, R. S., *A Guide Book of United States Coins*. Racine, Wis., Western Publishing Company, 1971.

Willem, J. M., *The United States Trade Dollar*. Racine, Wis., Whitman Publishing Company, 1965.

INDEX

299